MARVELLOUSLY MADE

A biblical tour around your body

Jim Parratt

TO JUNE.
THANKS FOR TODAY AND THE JOY
OF HAVING YOUR DAD AMONG
US AT THE HIGH KIRK..
EVERY BLESSING.
NORMAN @ JENNIFER

British Library Cataloguing in Publication Data:
a catalogue record for this publication
is available from the British Library

ISBN   978-1-871828-98-6

Typeset in 11.5pt Minion Pro at Haddington, Scotland

Printed by West Port Print & Design, St Andrews

CONTENTS

FOREWORD

There is a West African greeting – not 'how are you' (or even, as in Australia, g'day) but 'Ow de body'? If this small book had been written with such a readership in mind that might have been a good title for it. And the response to that greeting? 'De body fine!' But our bodies are more than 'fine'; as the psalmist wrote (Psalm 139:13,14) 'you (God) formed (shaped) my inward parts, knitted me together, we are fearfully and marvellously made'.

However, how often do we think about our own body except when something goes wrong with it? Yet all of our life is lived within this body of ours. We express wonder and amazement, and rightly so, about the universe(s), of which we are such a tiny part, but how often, I wonder, do we think of the marvel of that well-functioning body we inhabit, that 'miracle within'? After all, we could not manage without it! Thoreau was right when he wrote, 'talk of mysteries, I stand in awe of my body' whilst Einstein spoke of his 'rapturous amazement' of it.

How much do we know about our own body? And, do we have a 'longing to know' more? After all, Jesus himself had a body like ours; he too could smell and taste the food he ate, his digestive tract worked in the same way as our own, his heart rate increased as he climbed the Mount of Transfiguration, his blood shed on Calvary was the same as ours, carrying in life the same breathed-in oxygen to every cell in his body. He was fully human. Not just the incarnate Godhead 'veiled in flesh', he really was 'flesh and blood'. As we are.

Now the bible is full of words that relate to the functions of the body and of the things we do in it every day of our lives. We will look at some of them. It is as though I a physiologist, am taking a leisurely stroll through scripture; now and then a particular word has the capacity to stop me in my tracks and captivate my attention; a word with a physiological as well as a scriptural meaning. And then asking of that word – what does it mean, does an understanding of how this part of the body functions, shed light on its meaning in scripture?

My hope is that what is written will increase, even if just a little, your sense of wonder at the body you live in.

ACKNOWLEDGMENTS

Many thanks to Pauline Hoggarth, who first invited me to contribute to the writing of SU Notes ('Encounter with God') on the Old Testament book of Numbers, to Graham and Patricia Thorpe who introduced me, nearly forty years ago, to the writings (never surpassed) of the surgeon Paul Brand, writings which first set in motion the present thoughts about the body, to Susan Campbell for much help with the manuscript and for years as my 'laptop doctor extraordinary', to Dan Hough for ideas about the book cover, to my patient and understanding editor Jock Stein and lastly to those unsuspecting yet encouraging church congregations in various parts of the West of Scotland who, over the years, first listened to an exposition of some of the subjects outlined in the following pages; 'words spoken are both previous to and inherently superior to words written'.

This book is for my wife of sixty years Pam (Pamika),
who first showed me Jesus by life and word,
my children Stephen (with Fiona),
Deborah, and Jonathan (with Leigh),
my seven grandchildren Sharon (with Jordan),
Ailsa, Joshua, Kirsty, Daniel, Shona, Rebecca
and my great-granddaughter Alice Rose.

1 STANDING (and BALANCE)
'Stand still',[1] 'stand firm' in the faith[2]

There are at least eighteen different definitions of 'stand' in our English dictionaries and the Greek New Testament has nine different words so translated in the various English versions. The basic definition is straightforward; it is to remain in an upright position especially on one's feet, usually in a specified place and without moving. No wobbling or swaying and either with two feet together ('standing to attention') or with legs apart ('at ease'). Sometimes this also means, especially when elderly or very young, with some other means of support.

Physiologically, standing is quite complex and, of course, has to be learnt and under certain circumstances, relearnt. There is always excitement when the baby of the family first stands, initially holding on for support, and then for a few seconds, alone. After which, with swaying and a few wobbles, the baby flops to the floor. Surprise, tears perhaps and then laughter all round!

First, let us examine what is involved when, for example, a command is given to stand, 'be upstanding'. That request or command is first heard, which means that the auditory apparatus and the relevant parts of the brain are involved, and then acted upon. The feet are firmly planted on the ground and the body lifted to an upright position. This is achieved by muscle contraction of the lower limbs, pulling bones through their relevant attached tendons leading to the straightening of some muscles (extension) and the bending of the limb (flexion). However, receptors on the soles of the feet, the heels, calf muscles, ankles and hips are all involved. In order to do this the brain

---

1 Exodus 14:13
2 1 Corinthians 16:13

and spinal cord need information especially from the muscles themselves (the so called 'stretch receptors'), from the receptors in the muscle spindles and from proprioceptors (responding to touch and pressure) in the feet which give information about the state of the surface (even, firm, slippery, soft) on which the feet are placed. One has only to realise the complexity of this 'simple' procedure when one faces physical injury, either centrally within the brain (stroke) or more locally within the spinal cord or lower limbs. The author had to relearn how to stand after knee surgery, after which external support was initially required in the form of a frame or later a walking stick.

Standing, both physically and spiritually, is thus a question of balance. We take a position where opposing forces are equal, where the centre of gravity is above the support (the two legs). This is why it is easier to stand with legs apart (babies learn this naturally) and why standing for any period on one leg is precarious because the area of support (the ground) is small compared with the height of the centre of gravity above the feet. Under these conditions one can then 'feel' changes in the standing foot as muscular forces alter the position of the thrust exerted between the foot and the ground to compensate for, and resist, the inevitable swaying arising from the upper parts of the body.

Standing is more difficult when the ground shifts as, for example, standing on a moving escalator, a rolling ship, when the ground is slippery or on a moving Glasgow bus! One important part of the body concerned with the maintenance of an upright posture is the vestibular organ in the inner ear; this registers movement and angles of turn and orients us to gravity in order to tell us where we are physically in space. Tilting in one direction, to the side or forward or back, an accidental displacement in a particular direction, needs to be corrected by a corresponding displacement in the opposite direction achieved by adjusting, through muscular forces, the thrust exerted by the limbs. The instruction on escalators to 'hold on' makes good sense. It should be noted that 'toppling', which gives rise to the sensation of losing balance, is not the same as 'falling'. In falling the body compensates by thrusting out the other limb in the direction of the impending fall in a 'rescue operation'; this is to attempt to find a firm obstacle against which to develop an opposing force. Impairment of one's sense of balance and equilibrium is unpleasant as any airline steward pouring coffee to passengers during periods of turbulence knows only too well! Being securely balanced is important for our mental stability and enhances our sense of wellbeing.

Roberts in his book *Understanding Balance*[3] discusses the role of 'anticipatory pre-emptive actions' with reference to maintaining balance. These are voluntary actions, based on past experience, leading the body to anticipate the unstable effects of swaying and then compensate for them, all without the subject being aware of what is happening. Such a response is 'learned' and becomes habit even from an early age. It emphasises again the importance of balance in our physical lives.

There is another physiological effect of standing which also has implications for the scriptural command 'stand firm in the Lord'. This relates to the cardiovascular effects of suddenly standing and of maintaining this position for long periods. When moving from a sitting to an erect position, especially if this is performed rapidly, there is a fall in blood pressure, termed 'postural hypotension', which can lead to loss of consciousness and fainting. This is because the fall in blood pressure deprives the brain of an adequate blood supply. Postural hypotension is a particular problem for people on antihypertensive drugs for the treatment of high blood pressure. The explanation for this sudden fall in blood pressure is that, due to the effect of gravity, blood 'pools' in the now distended veins of the lower limbs.

This pooling of blood also occurs when standing for long periods, especially in hot weather. The author remembers a striking newspaper picture of soldiers fainting during a celebration of the Queen's birthday during an unusually hot July day. The

---

3   Roberts, T. D. M. *Understanding Balance*, Chapman and Hall, London 1995

photograph showed several soldiers lying on the ground having fainted. It seems that those who remained upright were the older soldiers who had learnt the trick of contracting their leg muscles to aid the return of blood to the heart and brain; and presumably all without the Queen noticing! The military authorities, who knew little of normal physiology, subjected those unfortunate, perhaps younger, fainting soldiers to extra periods of 'square bashing' to improve their fitness. It had nothing to do with fitness but was the normal physiological response to standing for long periods in hot weather.

Now, hopefully it should be clear that all the above have spiritual implications for 'standing firm'; complexity, learning (and relearning), balance and potential difficulties. For example, those 'anticipatory pre-emptive actions' referred to above, being prepared beforehand for those situations we know from past experience might throw us off balance. Thus, we might know from previous experiences that a particular situation could well be dangerous to go to because they were once 'places' of past failings. Best not to go there! 'Let him who thinks he stands take heed lest he fall'.[4] Dangerous to go out when there is ice underfoot. The traveller in a strange hotel is advised to check out the fire exit; too late when the alarm bell goes! Take heed. 'Mind the gap'.

Standing Firm

In God's word 'to stand' is a command and not an option and, just as in the vocal command to 'be upstanding', the scriptural command needs to be seen (read), heard (since ears and orientation are intimately linked), leading eventually to action (the response). All this first involves an understanding of what the original Greek word means; 'standing (to place oneself) on a firm foundation'. It is a military term (steko); a soldier stands firm, holding his position, standing up straight, well balanced,

---

4   1 Corinthians 10:12

preventing the opposition from gaining access. It is to remain upright and balanced over a long period. And, just as physical standing is complex, requiring information (so called 'sensory input') in order to determine where that standing body is in relation to space ('where I am') so too in the spiritual realm; we need to know where we are spiritually. We are to take up a firm, stable position rooted deep and grounded in Christ, trusting in him, hoping in him and secure in him; our stability is firmly grounded in God himself. Just as the psalmist testified, it is God himself who has 'set my feet on a rock and given me a firm place to stand'.[5] We certainly need this firm place because there are days in which we feel as turbulent as being adrift on the high seas; we need stability to help us navigate our way through the storms of life. We stand in Christ himself; as the hymn writer puts it 'I stand in Christ with sins forgiven'. He alone is the cornerstone. This secure standing comes then through faith in Christ – in who he is and what he has done; 'as far as your faith is concerned you are in a sound position', a firm place;[6] this faith comes through the grace of God,[7] 'this grace in which we stand' (hold our place).[8]

Sometimes to 'stand firm' is a plea rather than a command, a prerequisite for unity. The emphasis is on 'one', 'standing firm in one spirit', as one man, 'side by side' as in Paul's letter to the church at Philippi, written partly to counteract divisions within the fellowship. In a delightful insight into Paul's pastoral gifts it is only at the end of the letter that he comes around to the problem of division. He does this in a subtle, gracious way; after starting the letter with prayer (1:3-11) and the need for humility (2:2,4) then comes the plea to 'stand firm in the Lord' (4:1) before he again entreats unity (4:2,3).

---

5 Psalm 40:1-5

6 2 Corinthians 1:24; 1 Thessalonians 3:8

7 Ephesians 2:8

8 Romans 5:2

Standing Still

The invitation or command to 'be upstanding' is first an act of homage; as the psalmist puts it[9] 'we stand in awe of God' (we will all one day stand before him in judgement) and, in some churches, we stand when God's word is brought into church and placed on the pulpit. It is also an act of courtesy; we stand at weddings, funerals, for royalty, and for academic processions. At one time men stood when a woman entered the room; we stand in order to give a seat to an elderly or disabled passenger. In these situations we 'stand firm and stand still' as acts of courtesy.

In the story of Elijah in 1 Kings (chapters 17 to 19), following the dramatic encounter with the prophets of Baal and his subsequent flight from Jezebel, God commands Elijah to 'stand (still) on the mount before the Lord' at the entrance to the cave. It was here after the great wind and the earthquake, that Elijah heard God speaking to him in a 'divine whisper' (19:12). He had to be still and come close to God; the voice came softly, pianissimo (ppp) rather than treble forte (fff).

But how did this voice come? Trevor Hudson once suggested that it perhaps came 'in the form of distinctive thoughts with a certain 'feel' about them'. Whichever way it came it was a word of encouragement. Elijah's view of the situation was that he was a failure, 'let me die, take away my life' (19:4). He thought his work for the Lord was finished and that he was 'alone' (19:10) but God's take on the situation was that there is still work for him to do (19:15) and, he was not alone; there are others (9:18). It is when we are quiet, 'standing still', in the stillness and the silence, that God speaks to us. And, like Elijah, we have to make provision, time and place, to give God the opportunity to do this.

Just as physically we often need support from others (my wife when walking now needs my right arm as well as her stick!) so it is true spiritually that, if we are to stand firm, we need the support of others. Ultimately this is the Lord himself, 'God is able to make

---

9 Psalm 22:23

him stand'[10] 'because he is (close) at my right hand I shall not be moved.'[11]

There is a delightful story of Paul having, apparently unsuccessfully, preached the gospel to the Jewish Council[12] – being shouted down before he had hardly begun – it was at this point that 'The Lord stood by (meaning near or with) Paul.'[13] There was both the command to 'take courage' and the assurance that, despite the failure he felt, he really had testified to Jesus. Further, there was a promise that he would do so again in the future. Such a firm promise must have meant much to Paul at this time of disappointment and would surely have encouraged him in the delays, trials and anxieties in the years ahead.

So, the Lord stands with us. It is always so. He was standing close, near, even before we trusted in him; 'Behold I (Jesus) stand at the door and knock'[14] standing there before we even opened the door.

Usually however this support we need to 'stand firm' comes from God working through other people. Indeed, Paul himself said how this once came to him. It was after the Lord had met him on the Damascus road that 'one Ananias came to me' (standing with) and calling him 'Brother Saul.'[15] And how did this courageous and obedient Ananias 'stand with' him? By opening his eyes, sharing with him God's word, a word for Saul alone, and encouraging him by telling what God had in mind for him to do – 'you will be a witness for Jesus to everyone', his apostolic commission. So, we 'stand with' others in their times of disillusionment and distress by being with them (physical presence) and by sharing God's word, encouraging (or challenging) them through what God has said.

---

10 Romans 14:4

11 Psalm 16:8

12 Acts 23:1-10

13 Acts 23:11

14 Revelation 3:20

15 Acts 22:13

2 WALKING

'Keep on walking in the grace of God'[1]

The English language has two, quite different, meanings of the verb 'to walk'. It is both a physical activity (progress by lifting and setting down each foot in turn never having both feet off the ground at one time) and, figuratively, to 'live in a specified manner', signifying the whole round of activities of the individual life. The word is used in both these senses in English bibles especially in the second, somewhat archaic, sense in the King James version (AV). However, even in some modern translations, including Eugene Peterson's 'The Message', there are some places, in John's first letter for example, where even modern translators cannot escape using 'walk' meaning 'to live'. Of the six Greek words translated 'to walk' all except one are used to signify 'to live'. This double meaning of 'to walk' is not found in most other European languages as the author discovered to his cost when once speaking by interpretation, to a group of Hungarian medical students!

Walking is what we all do. It is the most natural physical activity, mastered within a few months of birth and which continues, if we are fortunate, to the end of our lives. On average, and depending on age and ability, we walk about 750 miles a year which means that, halfway through this year (2017), I have already walked as far as Glasgow is from Manchester. In a lifetime this means about 60,000 miles, the distance of several return trips from Scotland to Australia. And, for me all this with very little maintenance to the apparatus involved, except for one knee being replaced. Of course, this is an average distance; many walk during their lifetime considerably further.

As humans, we are almost uniquely equipped, by anatomical adaptation, to move by bipedal progression (capable of moving

1   Acts 13:43 (AV)

8

on two feet) with periods of double support of the body (both feet on the ground) alternating with single support (one foot on the ground, the other in the air). Sometimes, when walking very quickly, both feet can be off the ground for a fraction of a second; *pied en l'air*! Think, for a moment what happens when you begin to walk. After that decision to do so, and if one is 'right footed', that initial step ends with the right heel, then the whole foot on the ground. At this point the left foot is also (just) still on the ground, 'double support'. As the body moves forward the centre of gravity shifts to the front of the left toes and the weight of the body is now supported by the right leg ('single support'). The left leg then flexes and swings forward until that foot reaches the ground. We are now again in the phase of 'double support', both feet on the ground. And so on. Sounds complicated when one attempts to describe the walking motion in words! But just think about what you are doing when you take your next step!

So, although walking is a highly efficient form of locomotion it is physiologically very complex, involving about fifty different bones (a quarter of all the bones in our bodies) and a huge number of muscles all acting dynamically with the ground.

Now, how about walking in the spiritual sense of progress in the Christian life, living as a believer in the world? Let us recollect some of the passages in Scripture that use this as a description of the spiritual journey. Here are some examples. In Psalm 23 we have 'though I walk in the valley of the shadow of death' (or 'through the dark valley') whilst Job could say 'by his light I walk through the darkness'. We are to walk 'in the light of the Lord'.[2] Then in Micah, we are reminded that what the Lord requires of us is 'to love mercy, to do justly and to walk humbly with our God'[3] and to walk 'before God'[4] in this world of trouble.[5] This is taken up in the New Testament and, indeed,

2   Isaiah 2:5; Job 29:3

3   Micah 6:8

4   Genesis 17:1; 24:40; Psalm 56:13

5   Psalm 138:7

was a favourite metaphor of Paul. We can imagine him pacing around his prison cell, and stimulated by this walking, writing to the Ephesian church about walking in good works (2:10), in love (5:2), in faith (and not by sight)[6] and worthy of the Lord.[7] Compare also 'walking in Christ',[8] in newness of life,[9] 'honestly'[10] and 'after the Spirit'.[11] Negatively, we are not to 'walk after the flesh',[12] 'after the manner of men',[13] 'in craftiness',[14] 'in vanity of mind',[15] or 'in a disorderly manner'.[16]

However, it is in John's first letter that the use of the term is most apparent and it is interesting that even in modern translations (which translate most of the above Pauline references as 'live') the verb in 1 John is still translated 'walk' rather than 'live'. Thus, we are to 'walk' in the light[17] and not in darkness, in love, 'according to his commandments'[18] and, if we claim to live in Jesus, we must 'walk even as Jesus walked'.[19] We are then to 'keep on walking in the grace of God'.[20]

So, what is involved in physical walking that we can apply to walking in the spiritual sense?

---

6   2 Corinthians 5:7
7   Ephesians 4:1; Colossians. 1:10; 1 Thessalonians 2:12
8   Colossians 2:6
9   Romans 6:4
10 1 Thessalonians 4:12
11 Romans.8:4
12 Romans 8:4
13 1 Corinthians 3:3
14 2 Corinthians 4:2
15 Ephesians 4:11
16 2 Thessalonians 3:6
17 1 John 1:6,7
18 2 John 6
19 1 John 2:6
20 Acts 13:43

1. Walking Involves Coordination and Balance

Walking is physiologically very complex because it involves so many parts of the body – and not only the legs! It begins with the intention, the decision, or the 'command' to walk. This is the role of the cerebral cortex, which plans the activity and relies on 'feed forward' mechanisms based on sensory input from the eyes, ears, muscles, joints (especially from the hips) and from the skin and muscles, especially of the feet. This informs us as to where we are in relation to the environment, where we are 'in space'. Only recently has the discovery been made that there is a 'positioning system' in the brain, nerve cells that effectively form a 'map' of our immediate surroundings. These are cells that allow precise positioning making it possible for us to navigate our way, by walking, through a complex environment.

One simple student experiment to demonstrate the importance of this sensory input is to ask a 'volunteer' (?) to walk along a chalk line drawn on the floor. No problem! Even if blindfolded, most can manage this manoeuvre pretty well. But, still with a blindfold, if sensation from the feet is reduced by plunging them in very cold water, it is almost impossible to walk that straight line because there is now no input from the sensors in the feet. Interference with central control, for example following alcohol consumption, has a similar effect.

There is a sense then in which walking is a sensory experience because doing it means we are interacting with the external environment navigating our way through it. All five senses are brought into play, feeling (touch, we can 'feel' the ground despite the barriers, between the ground and the sensory endings in the soles of the feet, by socks and shoes), smell (from our surroundings as we walk – from the pine trees, gorse blossom or the petrol fumes from cars), hearing (the 'crunch' of our feet on a snowy path) and even sometimes taste (the salt on our tongues as we walk along the beach).

That it is the brain that controls this coordinated activity of the thousands of motor units involved in bipedal progression is demonstrated by studies in patients with spinal injury, for where the spinal cord is separated from the brain, walking is no longer possible. This shows that it is the discharge of motor neurons in the brain stem, down through the spinal cord (the 'final common path') that is responsible for the complex mechanisms involved in walking.

How does all this complex activity involved in physical walking relate to the spiritual activity of 'walking with God'? Like physical walking, although spiritual walking is, in one sense, natural and 'simple'. It is in essence, far from that! The spiritual walk first demands an active decision to begin to 'walk with Christ'. And, just as the act of physical walking depends upon sensory input, so too does walking with God. This comes through conversation with God, God speaking and us listening, through God's word and prayer. We cannot move forward with God without this and, just as in physical walking everything is together and well balanced, so too it should be in the spiritual walk. There must be balance between our private lives and our public lives, between our 'Sunday lives' and our weekday ones. No discrepancies, no mental compartments. No places in our minds and in our world where God is excluded. All of life together, beautifully balanced. The Christian walk may not be straightforward but it should be balanced, coordinated.

2. Walking Needs to be Learnt – and Sometimes Relearnt

It is fun watching babies learning to walk! Holding on and then letting go, with that look of determination, apprehension and alarm when they plop to the ground – yet again! This is accompanied by tears of frustration but, often, laughter. It is fun, this learning process! As the physiologist Sir Charles Sherrington put it 'each step is a stumble caught in time'. Then suddenly it all comes together and after a time they have forgotten all about that learning process. It has become natural. No need any longer to think about the 'how to'. It is interesting regarding this learning process that even small babies demonstrate what is, in essence, a 'walking reflex'. If babies are lifted under their arms such that their wee feet are just touching the surface of the ground they begin to make leg movements akin to walking. It seems to be inherent, part of them – and us.

For some, walking has to be relearnt for example following injury, stroke or after prolonged bed rest following an operation. Something happens to us and we have to start all over again and relearn to walk, thinking hard where to put our legs and then what happens next. Often, in such circumstances we need support, with frame or a stick or of the arm of a friend, else we stumble and fall. Coordination and balance go and, because as we have seen, walking is so complicated, many things can go awry.

Each of these aspects of walking, learning and relearning have spiritual parallels. In the Christian walk there are things that cause us to stumble and even fall, so that we have to relearn, almost restart the Christian walk. Paul wrote to the Galatian Christians, 'you were progressing (the word really means running) what caused you to stumble?'[21] They were not progressing in a straight path, not following the truth of the gospel; there were attempts to seduce them from their first faith by teachers who insisted that they must still keep the old laws. They were wandering off the path. These teachers said that there were things to be added to their primary faith in Jesus, circumcision for example. Faith is fine, they would say, but is not enough; other things (works) have to be added. They were teaching 'faith plus' for salvation.

There are other stumbling blocks of a different kind. There are hard, rocky places in a world where life in general terms is growing harsh for all and more pagan, the bastions of secularism and of militant humanism. To quote the Scottish theologian Ronald Wallace 'public opinion and the 'spirit of the age' are no longer, as they once were, allies we can trust to be on our side. Alongside Jesus, other names are called upon to bring us inspiration and

21 Galatians 5:7 GNV

13

salvation and many of our own attempts at renewal and recovery prove fruitless. Then, there is for many the stumbling block of 'science falsely so called'. The consequences are that Christians become less certain of their attachment to the substance of their faith. Faith is hindered, even destroyed 'when little academic minds with little heart for God niggle away at magnificent and precious realities'. It is under these circumstances that we might stumble and hence need support.

My wife, a few years ago, suffered a series of transient ischaemic attacks leading to cerebral injury needing support in walking. Even today, she needs that; stick in one hand, husband on the other arm! Lean on me! Paul in Galatians was aware of the need of support for those who were stumbling. He reminds us that we are to 'bear one another's burdens' and that we are to attempt to 'set right', but in a gentle manner, those who are losing their spiritual balance. We are indeed responsible for our own walk,[22] we are to 'keep an eye on ourselves'[23] but we are also to support, hold up and get alongside those who are finding the path rough. The Christian walk is not along a straight level path. There are occasions when there is no apparent way open before us and it is then that we need the support of others yet always believing that 'God will make a way where there seems to be no way'. Nothing around us will prevent God taking us to the destination we have sought and which He has planned.

Another stumbling block is the attitude and behaviour of other believers. Disagreements, arguments within the church community, splits, lack of love, lack of concern, the sense of being 'left out' and the folk, who should be in the forefront of caring for others, are sadly not. Such a lack of love and unity causes folk to stumble, especially the young; they then simply stop walking or may even go backwards. This is, in part, because we do not adequately prepare our young folk to deal with issues that can result in stumbling.

22 Galatians 6:5

23 Galatians 6:1 GNV

Suffering, to others especially, bereavement and redundancy are other causes of loss of balance. They are like potholes, or that gap between the train and the platform; we are to 'mind the gap'. A couple recently called to serve the Lord far from home were suddenly confronted, just two months after their arrival, with the news that the growth behind the eye of the wife's father was indeed malignant and had spread to other areas. 'We are dismayed by the news; it really shakes you up' was the comment; 'we really need your support and the Father's in this situation'.

General bodily wear and tear is a problem for walking especially as one gets older. Here the obstacle is not external; it is something within. Loss of lubrication, floating pieces of cartilage between joints, loss of muscle strength, irritation and pain, the increasing tendency of bones to fracture from falls, are all things resulting from changes within the body and are the normal result of ageing. These too have spiritual parallels. Or are the burdens we are carrying just too heavy? Many years ago when we left Nigeria the Scripture Union gave us at our farewell, an ebony carving. It is of two men. The one standing with the stick is blind; the smaller man, with legs terribly bent, sitting on the blind man's shoulders is lame. Apart, there are many things they cannot do. One cannot walk, the other cannot see. But together, supporting one another, they can both walk and see. They are complete. It is a picture of what support from a Christian fellowship should be like. In this case, because we would be three thousand miles apart, it is a picture of the support that results from praying for one another over vast distances.

Whenever we fall, as most of us do frequently, we need to get up and keep going. Sir George Solti, the Hungarian born orchestral conductor had as his motto 'keep going'. This was, so he said, the secret of his considerable success in life. That was Paul's message too for the believers at Antioch in Pisidia at the beginning of their spiritual walk. They were to 'keep going', and to 'keep on walking (continue) in the grace of God'.[24]

---

24 Acts 13:43 AV

3. Walking is Individual

No two people walk in the same way. How we do it is very individual. Indeed, gait recognition is part of the security system in several airports in India – the 'gait giveaway'! This is because there are subtle individual differences in bone (and tendon) length, in muscle strength, visual acuity, body mass and the centre of gravity, past injuries and 'personal style'. The position of the feet (one or other, or both, pointing in different directions, inwards or outwards or straight ahead), the swinging of the shoulders, the position of the head and hands, the 'roll' of the hips of Africans (or sailors). Just watch next time you go for a walk and are behind someone else! One friend, who spent years working among Chinese in Taiwan, still walks slowly with very tiny steps and on tiptoe. Just like those among whom she lived. And then there is how fast we walk. When I was 70 our younger son sent us a cassette tape entitled 'seventy things about dad', one of which was 'walks very fast'; sadly, no longer. However, if the speed may have gone, the urgency hopefully has not! As Charles Dickens wrote 'if I could not walk very fast and far I think I would explode and perish'!

The normal relaxed walking pace is about 3.3mph (around 4.2 feet/second). This gives a perfect balance between energy expenditure and conservation (recovery). This is because our leg muscles work better at this stride length and frequency. If we walk faster, or slower, than this our energy expenditure increases. Above about 4mph the stage of deliberate effort begins (the world record is about twice this) and energy wise is very uneconomical and far more exacting. On the other hand a lethargic saunter also does not provide efficient muscular contraction.

The Christian walk is also an individual walk. No one does it for us. Parents, wife, husband, grandparents, friend, pastor, church leader can support but cannot do the walk for us. We cannot be carried by someone else. We are responsible for our own relationship with Jesus, for our own 'walk' and, in the end, we will be held responsible.

4. Walking Means Progress; We have a Destination in View

We are not, as Christian believers walking 'on the spot' or in ever decreasing circles. There is a beginning and an end. 'Step by step we're moving forward' as the chorus goes. It is one step at a time because often we cannot see too far ahead. Essential news for those seeking guidance! As John Newman wrote as a prayer 'keep thou my feet; I do not ask to see the distant scene; one step enough for me'.

This walk is, for most of us, a long journey; some have been going slowly for some time. That long distance walk is also about discovering the true scale and complexity of the landscape – and discovering too about ourselves. This is particularly true of the older forms of long distance walking, especially of pilgrimage on foot with a spiritual destination in sight. Thus Abraham was called to leave Ur and 'walk by faith'[25] to a destination as yet unknown. He was instructed by God to simply 'walk before me'.[26] Psalms 120 to 134 (the 'songs of ascent' or 'degrees') are about journeys from different parts of the kingdom up to Jerusalem for one or other of the great Feasts of the Lord. These psalms traverse the experiences of our own spiritual pilgrimage of walking 'the Way'.[27] So this idea of pilgrimage, of walking 'the way', runs throughout Scripture. The 'how' is clear; we are 'to walk even as Jesus walked'[28] with our eyes 'fixed' on Him, 'looking to' Him[29], for He is 'the way',[30] not just a signpost for the way. The final destination is also clear; it is to be with Him in glory and to be 'like Him'.[31]

---

25 Hebrews 11:8, 9
26 Genesis 17:1
27 Acts 9:2; 19: 9, 23; 24:14; 2 Peter 2:2
28 1 John 2:6
29 Hebrews 12:1,2
30 John 14:6
31 1 John 3:2

5. Walking Means Effort; Energy is Involved

Of course, in any 'long walk' considerable effort is involved – and careful planning! Like walking the West Highland Way in Scotland, or the walk from Adelaide to the north coast of Australia by John Stuart (although much of that journey was by camel) or the man who walked the whole length of the Amazon river (and was bitten 50,000 times!). Even more painful and long was the forty year walk of the children of Israel in the wilderness. However, for the very few the promised land was eventually reached. Although all these were quite painful, long journeys, they were planned and the destination was clear. So with our own spiritual journeys; these too are often painful but they are also God planned. It is God himself who establishes, directs and 'keeps steady' our steps[32] and, with a clear end in view. A good journey needs a determined destination as well as an adequate means of travelling, sustenance for that journey and good companions. So it is for the spiritual walk.

6. Walking is Beneficial. It is 'Good to Walk'!

Did you know that simply walking for 30 minutes, two to five times a week without overexerting oneself, makes for a healthy body – and mind! We each have two doctors, a right leg and a left leg, always at our service. And no waiting! This thirty minute period can be broken down to, for example, three times ten minute periods. This is the advice from the British Heart Foundation. Walking makes a real difference to the maintenance of our overall physical health and quality of life. It results in a lowering of blood pressure, it tones up our muscles, strengthens our bones, wards off osteoporosis, reduces 'bad' (LDL) cholesterol (which is linked with heart disease) and elevates 'good' cholesterol (HDL). And, it helps to control weight. Further, it is free! Moreover, a recent United States report shows that walking improves our mental health, protects the brain from shrinking and preserves memory in the elderly. It is the 'magic pill 'which slows ageing,

---

32   Psalm 119: 133; Proverbs 16:9; Jeremiah10:23

reduces the chance of hip fractures (some say by as much as forty percent) and reduces cognitive decline. Further, the World Cancer Research Fund has shown that if people were to undergo more crisp walking it would help reduce breast and bowel cancer.

There is still debate regarding precisely how frequently and how much exercise is needed to protect the heart. These questions have exercised the group I have been working with for a number of years, where our particular emphasis has been on the precise biochemical mechanisms involved. Some of these results have been published elsewhere.

What is true of physical walking applies also to our spiritual walk; it really is beneficial and delightful[33] to keep moving in the Christian life. Of course, effort is involved; planning too. It is not an haphazard journey. Perhaps in our churches there are too many static Christians who seem to believe that little effort is required, or that they can simply be carried along from one Sunday to the next. We need to grow and keep moving. Standing still or stepping backwards do not lead to progress towards that ultimate destination of being like Jesus.

7. Walking Means Discovery – 'We have not Been this Way Before'

When Paul visited Athens for the first time[34] one of the first things he did was to walk around the city. It was a walk of discovery; a good way of getting to know a new place. The Christian walk is a 'voyage of discovery', an exploration. We each one tread a different path; no one's experience of life is the same as another's. Marriage or singleness, parenthood, indeed all the variety of life's experiences, involve exploration, getting to know place and person. Worship, that prime occupation of the spiritual life, is itself exploration. The Methodist minister, Fred

---

33   Psalm 37:23, 24
34   Acts 17:23

Pratt Green expresses this perfectly in his hymn 'God is here'. 'Here, the servants of the Servant, seek in worship to explore, what it means in daily living, to believe and to adore'. In other words, worship is also a preparation for living in the everyday world. And, what is true of worship is true of the whole of the Christian walk, a continuing discovery of new things about God and about ourselves It is exploration; none of us has walked this precise path before. Exciting!

8. We Walk in Company; We are Never Alone

Although to walk alone is, of course, possible the good walker knows that the great trek of life requires a companion. There is an African proverb which says 'If you want to go quickly go alone; if you want to go fast go together'. To interpret! When you go 'fast' (in company) you make more rapid progress than if you go alone ('quickly'); 'fast' is faster than 'quick'! Once many years ago in Nigeria my wife and I were travelling on a narrow sandy road when we were charged by a bush cow. We never discovered what damage the cow suffered but the car was disabled. It was getting dark and we were still some way from our destination. And, no mobiles in those days! In those circumstances one of the first things you do is pray! Minutes later we heard the sound of singing and a party of foresters came along, moving fast and with all the necessary tools to get us moving. Walking and singing go together and, it is best done in company. As a recent political slogan has it – 'better together'. Certainly, true of walking.

The Christian walk then is in company; it is a walk with God himself. We are told that Enoch and Noah 'walked with God'[35] and we too are to 'walk humbly with our God'.[36] The Lord never leaves us, never forsakes, and is always 'with'. God walks behind us, 'I will walk before the Lord in the land of the living',[37] we will hear his voice

---

35 Genesis 5:22, 24; 6:9

36 Micah 6:8

37 Psalm 116:9

behind us saying 'this is the way walk in it.'[38] Then, wonderfully God walks before us, he walks ahead; 'I the Lord walk before you.'[39] Before we get there, wherever or whatever that situation is, God is already there. So, we 'follow' (another great scriptural word). We, as a community of believers, 'walk in the steps of the faith',[40] 'keeping in step with Christ', in line, in step with the truth of the gospel.[41] Then, God is also alongside us on the walk; 'though I walk through the dark valley you are with me'.[42]

However, of the six New Testament words translated 'walk' perhaps the most wonderful is *emperipateo*; it means to 'walk about in' or among.[43] There is a similar expression in Leviticus 26:12 and in Deuteronomy 23:14, where God says 'I will walk among you' or 'I will live in them and I will be their God'. God is walking around in the lives of believers and in his church; Jesus walking in the midst of the churches.[44] What does he find I wonder? If this is true then every door of our lives must be open to Jesus. The King is in residence! Does this word throw light on the person of God himself I wonder? God is in three persons Father, Son and Holy Spirit, each voluntarily encircling, moving around the other two, pouring love, delight and adoration into each, a dynamic, pulsating walk (dance?) of joy.

Walking then is companionable. Walking in company hand in hand, arm in arm, sharing ideas, problems, worries, putting things in a wider perspective. This walking is a sharing, loving fellowship with our ever living, ever present Lord. This really is what the Christian walk is all about. We are to 'keep on walking in the grace of God'.

---

38 Isaiah 30:21
39 Exodus 23:23; 32:34
40 Romans 4:12
41 Galatians 2:14
42 Psalm 23:4
43 2 Corinthians 6:16
44 Revelation 2:1

3 RUNNING

'Let us run with endurance the race that is set before us'[1]

To run is to move rapidly over the ground by using each foot alternatively. We are built to do this! In contrast to walking, running involves a 'bouncy' or 'pogo stick' mode' of transportation. The heel and toe progression of walking becomes uneconomical; in running the tendons and ligaments of our legs are the key factors, acting as elastic springs which then return back to their original shape. This stretching, contraction and recoil releases the energy involved; it is therefore tendons rather than muscles that do the considerable work involved, the pushing off the ground (the 'ground force'). Running is strenuous, involving a significant increase in the amount of oxygen we extract from the air we breathe, increases in heart rate as well as the output of the heart at each beat (the stroke volume) and a tripling of the amount of blood going to the lower limbs.

Of course, we all run in different ways. Like walking it is individual. Perhaps none more so than the Scottish athlete, Olympic 400m gold medallist and then missionary in China, Eric Liddell. He ran in a rather peculiar way, and one certainly not found in the coaching manuals. Towards the end of his races he held his head held high looking upwards and with joy; 'God made me fast' he said, 'And when I run, I feel his pleasure!'! When a play was made of the competition between Liddell and the 100m Olympic champion Abrahams, the actor playing Liddell found his mannerisms hard, and dangerous, to perform on stage; he could not see where he was going!

There are different techniques involved in running at speed. Jogging around the streets for exercise is quite different to long distance (marathon and ultramarathon) running, when we 'push

---

1   Hebrews 12:1

ourselves' long and hard and 'through the wall' of that physical and psychological barrier which makes runners wobble and when the body says 'no more'. But is this weariness of the limbs only or of the mind? In contrast, the explosive force required in sprinting is quite different, with enormous force generated out of the blocks. Exhilarating! There are perhaps few other physical activities like the sheer pleasure associated with running the inside bend of a 200m race. Just like flying! Incidentally in sprinting the metabolic rate (energy expenditure) is more than ten times that involved in running a marathon and just ten seconds of high speed running corresponds to the calorific value of about ten grams of glucose. In contrast, the energy expenditure during walking is about three to four times that of sitting and rather less than twice that of standing.

Running is a word often used in scripture. Often it simply means physical running of the kind described above. For example, on the day of the resurrection the two disciples, Peter and John, ran together to see for themselves that the tomb was empty. Both of them ran although the 'other disciple' (John) was the faster; he 'outran Peter'.[2] People were so eager to hear what Jesus was saying that they too ran to get a good place to see.[3] Zacchaeus had to hurry ('he ran')[4] to get a good view of Jesus; Rhoda was so surprised to hear Peter's voice at the door that she too ran to those praying inside.[5] Mark, whose gospel is so full of movement (the words often seem to 'run into one another') is particularly fond of the word (*trecho* in Greek).

However, in scripture 'to run' can also refer to 'the exceptional demands of life as compared with 'walking', which is akin to the ordinary 'daily grind'. This is the meaning of 'they who wait on

---

2   John 20:4

3   Mark 6:55; 9:15; 10:17

4   Luke 19:4

5   Acts 12:14

the Lord shall run and not be weary';[6] so, in a spiritual context to run means to wait! The Christian race is like a marathon rather than a sprint, although there may well be times during that race when the pleasure, excitement and exhilaration of running is like sprinting. We can 'run fast' spiritually! However, most of the time the spiritual race is more like a marathon; there is an end in sight, a destination. This is so unlike the recent and increasingly popular sport of 'ultra-running', where the object is to run around a 400m running track for 24 hours (with occasional stops for drinks and food). The current record is 160 miles. All without going anywhere!

Running then in scripture, used metaphorically, is an appropriate description of the Christian journey. This is a race we all run and for which we all have to train. We do not succeed simply by turning up at the starting line! It is to be run with faith, patience, self-control and perseverance[7] and with the end in sight.[8] Paul's fear for himself and for others, one that is also ours perhaps, is that the race might be run in vain[9] because our progress is somehow hindered. To the Galatian Christians Paul wrote[10] 'you were going (running, past tense) so well, who hindered you in your present running', literally 'what tripped you up', in this case from 'obeying the truth'? I remember as a small boy during WW2 seeing my father, a good athlete and on leave from the army, take part in a distance race included in our annual village fete. Out of sight of the judges his chief rival the village 'champion', a young farmer, purposely 'cut in' tripping my father up and pushing him out of the race. It is a picture of what can happen in the spiritual race; something, or more usually someone, by word or attitude, obstructing others in their

---

6   Isaiah 40:31

7   1 Corinthians 9:24-26; Hebrews 12:1

8   2 Timothy 4:7

9   Galatians 2:2; Philippians 2:16

10   Galatians 5:7

individual race. Young believers seem especially vulnerable and Jesus had a warning to their elders about this!

In this race we need the help of others. I saw recently on the TV an example of this. Two brothers, world champions at this event, were at the end of a triathlon, almost at the finishing line, when one of them became disorientated and ran off the track, clearly not knowing where he was. In his obvious confusion, his brother, running just behind him, saw his distress, put an arm around him and helped him over the line. Good to have a brother like that! Rather like in the 1992 Barcelona Games when the English quarter miler Derek Redmond pulled up near the finishing line with a hamstring injury and crumpled to the track in pain. As he hobbled towards the finishing line his father, in the crowd, scaled the restraining wall and reached his son. Leaning on his father's shoulder they crossed the line together. The entire crowd stood and cheered the two men! Is it, I wonder, when we are near the spiritual finishing line that, through age and infirmity, spiritually hobbling, we too are more in need of the help of others.

Of course, the spiritual race involves not the legs but the heart. It is not a fight to get out of bed but to trust in God. This race can be won flat on our backs; it may be run better by an invalid, flat on his (her) back than by an able self-sufficient person. This race is for the sick in body as well as for the physically healthy. One day perhaps we too will be on our backs, not even able to read the bible, almost unable to pray, mind and memory failing. It is especially then that we need the help of others, holding us up in prayer, helping us to run.

Individual spiritual journeys are, for most of us, long and arduous; there are exceptional demands. Quite often we meet times on that journey that are akin to the 'pain barrier' observed in physical long distance running. We hit a spiritual 'wall'; the pain of our present circumstances, personal for us (serious illness, bereavement, family or church breakups, loneliness) is too much for us. Can we continue? For the long distance runner the answer is to 'run through the 'pain barrier'; when this is done the pain lessens. The spiritual answer for the long run is similar. Despite the anguish of the circumstances, whatever they might be, with God's help, usually mediated through others, we can break through the barrier and continue to the end. We are to persevere determined, in the apostle Paul's words[11] to 'press on' forgetting what lies behind, straining forward to what lies ahead'. The important thing is that we finish!

There is the story of John Akwani, a marathon runner from Tanzania, who finished last in the 1968 Mexico City Olympic Games one hour after all the other competitors had completed the race. Still in great pain he was asked why he had continued to run to the end when he was so far behind. His reply? 'My country sent me here not simply to start the race, they sent me here to finish'. We might apply that to the Christian marathon; having started our spiritual journey with Christ we are to continue 'to the end', surrounded by that 'great crowd of witnesses'[12] looking to Jesus for the strength we need. As Jesus himself said, 'it is he who continues to the end who will be saved'.

11 Philippians 3:14
12 Hebrews 12:1

4 BREATHING

'The breath of the Almighty gives to me life'[1]

Once seen on a Brodick (Isle of Arran) garage wall: 'Customers help themselves to air'. Good idea and not only for customers! This is because the intake of air, and its vital constituent oxygen, is essential for, and synonymous with, life itself.

Breathing is a mechanical process involving the intake of oxygen contained in the air around us. It lasts as long as life itself. From that puzzled look on the baby's face after it has taken its first breath, forced to draw in that marvellous air for the very first time, to the final braying gasp at the end of life. Life enters us as we take that initial breath and leaves us when we breathe our last. If we attempt to deny its entrance into the body, if we hold our breath, then the face becomes blue, the neck veins engorge and we are literary fighting for breath. Although it lasts only for minute or so it feels like eternity. Frightening! Wonderful then that there are bodily systems in place to make sure we do not stop breathing completely.

Life is dependent upon breathing because all the cells of our bodies need oxygen in order to survive. We do this, in and out, with unremitting regularity, about ten to fifteen times a minute, less when sleeping and much more during exercise. This means that during an average lifespan of say eighty years we have breathed in (inspiration) and out (expiration) about four hundred million times. So many of these operational cycles over a life time without us thinking too much about it! What is supplied to the body through breathing is invisible and almost intangible yet, through this simple life giving act the body renews its vitality moment by moment. If respiration were to be discontinued we would be just minutes away from death. But what is in this air we breathe? What are its material properties that sustain life?

---

1   Job 33:4

Shortly after the restoration of the monarchy and the start of the reign of Charles II, the newly formed Royal Society in London examined this particular problem. Robert Hooke showed that an animal with an open chest could be kept alive by 'artificial respiration', that is when fresh air was blown into the lungs from a pump. Hooke also showed that the blood coming from the lungs was bright red but only if the artificial respiration was maintained; if it was stopped the blood became purple. In other words, blood changed colour on exposure to the oxygen containing air. Indeed, years before John Mayow (born in 1643) by 'hypothesis, deduction and experimentation' had discovered oxygen in all but name when he showed that he was able to maintain life by moving air in and out of the lungs (ventilation) as a result of lifting the ribs by contraction of the muscles between them. This expansion and contraction of the lungs, resulting from the movement of the chest wall, was dependent on the fact that the lungs are suspended in an airtight box. If there is a hole in the chest wall and air is admitted (creating a pneumothorax) the lungs would collapse.

During the act of inhaling (inspiration) the diameter of the thorax is increased whilst the muscular diaphragm at the floor of the chest flattens, allowing the capacity of the chest cavity to increase. When this muscular activity ceases at the end of inspiration the lungs are 'squeezed' by the ribs and the diaphragm returns to its position before the fresh intake of breath.

These respiratory cycles occur without conscious attention; we seldom think too much about breathing. Such automatic mechanisms are controlled by the lower brain stem connecting the thorax with the respiratory centre in the brain. In trauma conditions in which the neck is 'broken', these 'bellows' are immobilised and the subject then becomes dependant on a mechanical respirator, a ventilator.

Breathing is highly automated and regulated by information from 'sensors' (called 'chemoreceptors') which respond to changes in the blood concentration of oxygen and carbon dioxide. The supervisory centre in the brain itself contains such sensors. They are stimulated when the blood oxygen concentration is lowered or when the carbon dioxide levels are increased. In exercise for example, bodily oxygen demand is increased by the exercising muscles. This in turn lowers the blood oxygen content and increases the amount of blood carbon dioxide and blood acidity. The result is an increase in the rate and depth of respiration and thus in the pulmonary uptake of oxygen.

Normal respiratory cycles can be overridden for example during speech and singing and, for a limited time, by 'holding one's breath'. This is why breathing deeply before swimming enables us to stay longer underwater; it results in a lowering of the blood concentration of carbon dioxide which is a powerful stimulator of these chemoreceptors.

Now, for a little gentle physics! The amount of air breathed in with each normal, quiet effortless inspiration (eupnoea) is only about 10% of normal lung air capacity (total lung capacity, TLC – not to be confused with tender loving care!) which is about 5 litres. Increases in respiration occur when the air concentration of oxygen is reduced, for example at altitude. This is the reason why we are compelled to breath more frequently and more deeply the higher we climb. For example, a reduction in the concentration of oxygen in air of about 40% occurs at a height of around 3000m. At sea level, normal air pressure is about 760mmHg which means, since air contains about 20% oxygen, that the inspiratory partial pressure of oxygen is about 150mmHg. At 3000m this is reduced to about 100mmHg whilst at an altitude of 5500m (the highest for permanent human habitation) the inspired partial pressure of oxygen is only about 70mmHg, about half of that at sea level. A person not acclimatized to this altitude can only just tolerate this level without losing consciousness. This is why at such altitudes the heart rate is increased; to around 120 beats/minute, about twice that at sea level. Those living permanently at these high altitudes, in the Andes or Himalayas for example, or who become acclimatized at altitude, such as athletes training in Kenyan highlands, also have a marked increase in circulating red blood cells, thus increasing the oxygen carrying capacity of the blood. This enables the amount of oxygen delivered to the tissues to be maintained even at these altitudes.

In contrast, divers work at higher than normal atmospheric pressures. These conditions can be simulated experimentally in a hyperbaric chamber, allowing oxygen to be delivered at higher partial pressures. The author worked for several years in one such chamber at Glasgow's Western Infirmary. The question was to determine whether it was possible to increase the oxygen supply to the heart under conditions of decreased coronary blood flow. This was in order to 'salvage' dying cardiac cells by providing them with more oxygen. Breathing 100% oxygen at twice normal atmospheric pressure (2ATA) increases the partial pressure of oxygen to more than 1000mmHg. Contrast this with 100mmHg when ventilating with air at normal atmospheric pressure (1ATA). The main use for these chambers at that time (the mid 1960s) was in the treatment of coal gas poisoning. Not much need for that now. There is apparently a more recent 'use'; the tennis player and former world number one, Novak Djokovic apparently spends time in a hyperbaric chamber, presumably to increase his oxygen uptake. But how long does this increase last I wonder? And, as I write he has just been beaten in the second round of the 2017 Australian Open!

Of course, it is vital to slowly reduce decompression when returning to normal pressure otherwise, if the pressure within the chamber is reduced too quickly, dissolved gases are given off into the tissues as bubbles commonly known as the 'bends. These 'bubbles' can obstruct blood flow to organs such as the heart and brain.

What happens, and under what conditions, when breathing becomes more difficult? The simple answer is that this occurs when there is an obstruction inside or outside the respiratory tract. Imagine, for example, you choke on your food such that 'it goes down the wrong way', into the trachea rather than the oesophagus. This must be coughed up immediately because otherwise it can lead to suffocation and later to infection. When this occurs there is swelling around the obstruction leading to a persistent cough as the body does its best to remove the obstruction. The other form of obstruction comes from pressure on those light and airy lungs from outside. This is because the lungs are surrounded by a double-layered smooth membrane called the pleura, one surface of which is attached to the lungs, the other to the chest wall. Infection and inflammation of the pleura (pleurisy) makes the movement of the layers of the pleura over one another more difficult. This becomes painful and makes breathing more difficult due to pressure on the lung tissue from outside.

There are other conditions that make breathing more difficult. Indeed, of the most frightening of all emergences is to be called to someone who is not breathing (apnoea) or to asthmatics 'fighting for breath'. Are they breathing? Do they have a pulse? These are the vital signs of life because, as we have seen, life itself depends on an adequate delivery of oxygen to, and the removal of carbon dioxide from, the cells of the body. Failure to breath leads, within a few minutes, to tissue death, especially of those 'vital' centres such as the heart and brain which can only survive for a very short time before damage begins to occur. The first priority is to maintain an open airway; the 'aide memoire' for cardiopulmonary resuscitation is ABC (airway, breathing, circulation). Ventilation, by breathing into the lungs, is achieved by insufflation, blowing air into the lungs. The easy way to achieve this is by mouth to mouth resuscitation. The nostrils are pressed together with thumb and forefinger for about five seconds at a time and air blown into the lungs through the mouth. This provides an adequate level of blood oxygen of about 95%. If the heart has stopped beating then there is an urgent need for cardiac massage since, if cardiac arrest occurs, breathing ceases in less than one minute. Mechanical devices, used for example in gas anaesthesia, supplies air through a tube inserted into the trachea (intubation) or, in cases of infantile respiratory paralysis, by means of a 'tank respirator' or 'iron lung'.

Now, here is an interesting question which could well be in your mind. It is this. How is it that gaseous oxygen in the lungs can enter blood, in solution and then bound to the haemoglobin in red blood cells, since liquid and air must be kept in their separate compartments? The answer is because of the wonderful structure of the respiratory tract. This can be visualised as an inverted 'tree', the trunk being the trachea which begins in the glottis (the opening of the vocal cords) and ends in the upper part of the chest. It then divides at a Y folk (the carina) into smaller tubes (the bronchi) and then further subdivides into smaller and smaller branches, the bronchioles. These themselves terminate in tiny air sacs (three hundred million of them) called alveoli. These are akin to the small branches and leaves of a tree.

This parallelism between alveolar structure and the leaves of a tree is indeed close because, just as leaves 'breathe' and give out oxygen, so too do the delicate lung cells take up, 'breathe' oxygen from the inspired air (which is then released into the circulating blood); in return carbon dioxide is taken up from the blood and expelled from the lungs during expiration. This exchange is possible because of the close proximity of the single layer of epithelial pulmonary cells (which if spread out would cover an area of about a hundred square yards, about the leaf coverage of a young oak tree!) and the single layer of cells in the capillary blood vessel wall.

This maximises exposure to air allowing oxygen to easily pass from the lungs into the capillary blood and carbon dioxide to pass down a concentration gradient from the blood into the alveolar air sacs. This gas exchange is very rapid, converting the venous, carbon dioxide rich blood, into arterial, oxygen rich blood. The oxygen combines with the haemoglobin in red blood cells (or corpuscles) to form oxyhaemoglobin. There are about five million of these cells in each cubic centimetre of blood each of which carries over 250,000,000 haem molecules. In the tissues oxyhaemoglobin releases oxygen to the cells and is converted back to haemoglobin. Because haemoglobin can also combine with carbon dioxide this is carried to the lungs where it is given off in the expired air. What a transport system this is! We are indeed 'marvellously made'!

This gift of breathing is from God. He 'gives to all life and breath'.[2] In God's hand is 'the breath of all mankind', of 'every living thing'.[3] 'The Spirit of God has made me and the breath of the Almighty has given me life'.[4] He is the life-giving Spirit.[5] For those who have worked on a labour ward, and have seen many babies born, it is that first breath, sometimes scary, that never fails to excite. That look of surprise on the face of the newly born! In the mother's womb, well-nourished and warm, all it's needs are supplied, but then, once born, it is on its own as far as the supply of life-giving oxygen is concerned. For that 'life of its own', the baby needs to breath, a new experience; they have never done that before! So, 'let everything, and everyone, that hath breath praise the Lord'.[6]

Just as there is no life possible without spontaneous, or artificial, respiration so it is that there can be no spiritual life without breathing the breath that comes from God. God formed man and breathed into his nostrils[7] the breath of life such that the man became a living creature.[8] A wonderful example of 'mouth to mouth respiration', resuscitation even! It speaks of face to face and warmly personal intimacy, a proclamation of God's love because it is an act of giving. It is this breath, Spirit, that places us into a living relationship with our creator God making the essential difference between humans, made in the image of God, and other creatures. Breath is used throughout scripture to describe the

---

2 Acts 17:25
3 Job 12:10
4 Job 33:4
5 2 Corinthians 3:6
6 Psalm 150:6
7 Genesis 1:27
8 Genesis 2:7

life-giving capacity of God. It is God's in-breathing, inspiration, that gives life to man.

The Hebrew word for breath ruach, literally means 'air from breathing' and comes nearly four hundred times in the Old Testament. It is also the same word for wind coming, in this sense, in Genesis 3:8 where it means a 'refreshing evening breeze'. The same word can also mean a 'strong, constant wind'[9] or a gale, a tornado[10] or even that hot, rushing desert wind that scatters the sand. There is a similar parallelism between wind and spirit in the New Testament where the same word (pneuma) is used for both. For example, in Acts where, on the day of Pentecost, 'there came from heaven a sound like a rushing mighty wind',[11] like a gale, a seemingly a natural phenomenon both in origin and character. It was after this that the disciples were all 'filled with the Holy Spirit'. Just as in Ezekiel[12] when the wind blew upon those dry bones, unseen but mightily effective and filling them with new life, so too at Pentecost. There is a similar allusion in John's gospel where Jesus likens the natural wind blowing 'where it may' to everyone who is 'born of the Spirit'[13] the 'breath of a quiet whisper'. Or, as the Scots version has it, 'an ye hear the souch o it, but whaur it comin frae, an whaur it is gaein til, ye kenna'. Like the wind, the Spirit of God, is working in the life of a man, often through the 'God breathed out' Scriptures.[14] Invisible yes, but you can clearly see its effects.

To sum up, the Greek word (*pneuma*) denotes physical wind, breath or breathing, what we all do minute by minute, and the Holy Spirit (the 'breath of God'). However, it can also mean that invisible, immaterial part of man, his nature, his whole human personality, as in the final request of Stephen 'Lord Jesus receive my spirit', that is

---

9 As in Exodus 10:13, 19
10 Jeremiah 4:11
11 Acts 2:2
12 Ezekiel 37:9-14
13 John 3:8
14 2 Timothy 3:16

receive my life itself.[15] Indeed, so frequent is the use of (pneuma) in scripture that sometimes it is hard to tell whether it refers to spirit (in the sense of personality) or to the Holy Spirit (with a capital S). Yet, in all these contexts breath means life.

At a recent thanksgiving service for a friend the message was from the second chapter of Ecclesiastes - 'the day of death is better than the day of birth'. It raised this question. Which is better, our first breath or our last? Of course, for all of us there comes this 'final breath'. Charles Wesley's prayer was that he might use this to 'proclaim Christ the Lamb'. Yet this final breath, which ends life here on earth, moves us to that place, which Christ has prepared for us, where with some form of 'mysterious breath' we can continue to offer to God our praise in song. So indeed, 'let everything that has breath praise the Lord'.[16]

---

15   Acts 7:59

16   Psalm 150:6

5 EATING

'Your words were found and I ate them, the delight of my heart'[1]

Eating, regularly and from a varied diet, is a physiological function essential to physical vitality and survival. Similarly, feeding on Christ and on God's word is vital to our spiritual wellbeing. As Jesus said, 'whoever feeds on me shall live';[2] we are to 'feed on Him' and on God's word, the Scriptures.

Invitation

Eating begins with an invitation. The call - 'the food is on the table come and get it!' or that written or oral invitation to join with others around the dining table for food, drink and conversation. The process first involves preparation by the body to receive that meal. Then comes the ingestion of the food, we 'take' it in. This is followed by the digestive process, the absorption of the resultant breakdown products and finally, and hopefully, the satisfaction of time well spent. We are replete!

First is the decision as to what to eat! We need a 'balanced diet'. Much has been written about the best kinds of food and how to prepare them; witness the multitude of books and TV programmes on cookery. For babies, who rarely require an invitation to feed, it is milk, the supreme balanced food containing all that is necessary for growth and development. With weaning, the diet is expanded to include food and drink other than breast (or infant formula) milk, with a mixed diet from about six months.

A good balanced diet is of supreme importance for the maintenance of good health and indeed for life itself. It must contain adequate amounts of protein, essential fatty acids,

---

1   Jeremiah 15:16

2   John 6:57

minerals and vitamins, fibre, fruit and vegetables; a diet low in saturated fat and salt. It should provide all we need for growth, development and the energy requirements of daily activities.

Associated with 'what' to eat is the 'when' to eat. There are rituals involved. These include not only the invitation itself ('come') but the particular utensils needed for a particular diet and the appearance of the table. The 'when' is important because there are daily variations (called circadian rhythms) in the digestive processes which prepare the body, ahead of time, for the tasks involved in eating. So, for example, a regular pattern of three meals a day sets the relevant 'body clocks'. Anyone who has travelled across several time zones knows just how long it takes for the body to adjust to these time changes; the gastrointestinal tract is particularly slow in this respect.

Preparation

Before we begin to eat indeed, whilst we are still anticipating that delicious meal, the body is preparing to receive that food. It does this in several distinct ways. Two famous experimental studies were the first to demonstrate this. The Russian physiologist Ivan Pavlov, using experimental animals (usually dogs) created 'windows' through which he could observe the secretions of the stomach (and other parts of the gastrointestinal tract). These secretions could be then collected and analysed. He did this by bringing the stomach out through the body wall, with the blood and nerve supply intact, in order to observe its function under near normal conditions. He found that simply showing these dogs meat caused the release of gastric juice even before the beginning of ingestion; indeed, almost half of the maximum secretion by the stomach was released before food entered it. This stimulation of gastric secretion could also be achieved by linking the sight, and smell, of food with a learned oral stimulus such as the ringing of a bell, an example of a so called 'conditioned reflex'. Clearly then, the higher centres of the brain were involved in this anticipatory response.

However, the other piece of experimental evidence came even earlier, in the 1820s. This was from studies by an army surgeon William Beaumont. One of his patients, Alexis St Martin, had survived a gun-shot wound leaving him with a hole, or fistula, connecting his stomach with the exterior. Beaumont was able to collect multiple samples of gastric juice and was able to show that secretion could be stimulated by the sight and smell of food; venison was especially powerful in this respect!

Even the thought of food can bring about a desire to eat. This originates in that part of the brain concerned with emotion and 'reward'. Yet even to say that appetite 'starts in the brain' is an oversimplification because chemical substances produced in the mouth, stomach and intestines, especially a small peptide called ghrelin, are released into the blood stream and carried to the hypothalamus area in the brain where they act as appetite stimulants. There is an interesting time course involved; the release of this 'chemical soup of signals' is maximal just before the commencement of the meal. In summary then, the body prepares itself for eating; the 'triggers' for this anticipatory preparation to 'receive' food involve the time-dependent release of chemicals from the alimentary tract as well as messages to the brain from receptors in the eyes and nose; the sight and smell of enticing food.

Digestion

The body is now in a position to begin the process by which food is broken down into relatively simple chemical substances; in the mouth saliva begins to flow, even before food is in contact with the inside of the mouth, and this begins digestion. This is aided by chewing (mastication). The resultant particle size produced depends on early training and the nature of the food. As the tongue moves the food around the mouth the crushing force exerted can be considerable; over a hundred pounds of pressure is exerted by the incisors and molars, higher still if certain nuts are involved.

The bolus of food is then propelled into the oesophagus, a mainly voluntary process, and thence into the stomach. This is a bag like structure with a capacity of about a couple of pints. Here, the digestive process continues and the food is well mixed, due to the activity of the muscles of the stomach wall, with enzymes such as pepsin which breaks down protein and which works more effectively in an acid environment. This gastric brew is very powerful. These digestive processes take place without taxing the brain and occur involuntarily due, in part, to the activity of the 'brain within the belly', an intricate web of nerve cells within the stomach wall that control how long the food remains within the stomach. The bolus, now called chyme, is then moved along the alimentary tract where it is further broken down, by enzymes from the liver, pancreas and the intestine itself, into smaller constituents such as sugars, amino acids, small peptides, inorganic ions and vitamins.

Absorption

Although the mechanisms for the absorption of these smaller food constituents from the lumen of the intestine are complicated, the end result is that these substances are 'transferred' across the intestinal wall into the blood stream and then carried to other parts of the body. Because of the unique arrangement of the blood circulation to the intestinal tract the products of ingested food are taken first to the liver where they are further broken down and metabolized. It is also here that various proteins, with a wide range of important functions, are synthesised from the amino acids that resulted from the breakdown of proteins in the diet. The liver is thus a major manufacturing site for those chemical substances necessary for the life and activity of each body cell. Further, the liver has a protective function by breaking down potentially harmful substances (such as ammonia and certain drugs) into non-toxic compounds.

Food spends only an hour or two in the stomach and somewhat longer in the small intestine. What is left after absorption passes, in liquid form, to the large intestine where it remains for several hours. This is to allow water to be absorbed; astonishingly this can amount to about two gallons daily.

The entire process outlined above is slow; the transit time from the intake of food in the mouth to the elimination of waste products in the faeces takes around two to three days. It is longer in women than in men, and increases in both with age.

Spiritual Implications

Each of the above (invitation, preparation, digestion and absorption) has spiritual parallels. It matters what we eat and how we eat! We can compare then the physical act of eating, in order to sustain bodily health, with the feeding on God's word for our spiritual wellbeing and vitality. Both are essential for our survival. Just as, in order to live, food ingested and absorbed provides strength for normal physical activity[3] so too, for spiritual health, we need to 'consume' God's word (and Word). We are not to eat the bread of idleness[4] or the fruit of lies[5] or spend money, waste our resources and effort, on that which is not truly bread[6] and do not satisfy.[7] As Jesus himself said, it is written[8] 'man shall not live by (material) bread alone but by every word that proceeds from the mouth of God'.[9] there is bread which sustains spiritual life, which does for our spirit what wheaten or rye bread does for our body. This spiritual bread is to be sought for, kept, stored in the heart and not forgotten.[10]

All this begins with the invitation 'come'! Think, for example, of the invitations to the 'wedding feast' in Matthew's gospel (22:1-

---

3   1 Samuel 28:22

4   Proverbs 31:27

5   Hosea 10:13

6   Isaiah 55:1, 2

7   Isaiah 55:2

8   Deuteronomy 8:3

9   Matthew 4:4; Luke 4:4

10   Psalm 119:2,4,8,11,16

14), 'invite as many as you find' or of the invitation to the great banquet described in Luke's gospel, 'come, for everything is now ready'.[11] Then there is the gracious invitation in Isaiah 'come everyone, come buy and eat, listen and eat what is good, delight yourselves in rich food'.

The above ('feast', 'everyone') emphasises the communal associations with eating. The Jewish emphasis, for example, on the family meal with its relaxed (sometimes!) far ranging conversations, not the hurried 'eat up and get up' of most family meals. We eat in company with others. Then there is the gracious invitation every time we meet for the communion service or Lord's supper, to 'come' to the table with the call to 'take' and to eat. In the accounts in the gospels of the last supper[12] it was as the disciples were eating the Passover meal[13] that Jesus 'took the bread' blessed it, broke it, gave it and said take 'this is my body, do this in remembrance of me'. We should note that both 'take' and 'do' are commands. This was something Jesus 'earnestly desired to do' in the company of his disciples.[14] All this was in the context of 'normal' eating, here the regular annual Passover meal.

Wonderfully too there is the future invitation, again to eat, come 'to the marriage supper of the Lamb, gather for the great supper of God', a celebration of the marriage of Christ with his church, his spiritual bride.[15] Everything is ready, prepared and the invitation has been given. In the meantime, there is the promise that when we come to Christ, having accepted this so gracious invitation, he will 'come in and eat with' us[16] an invitation to a full, family life with the Lord involving conversation and sharing.

---

11   Luke 14:16,17

12   Matthew 26:17-29; Mark 14:17-26; Luke 22:14-30; John 13:1-30

13   Matthew 26:17; Mark 14:16, 22

14   Luke 22:15

15   Revelation 19:6-9, 17

16   Revelation 3:20

After the invitation comes the decision, as with physical eating, of what to eat. What are the essentials for spiritual eating? There seem to be two components of the spiritual diet, related but perhaps also distinct. The first comes in John's gospel and is described as a 'hard saying', hard probably in the sense of difficult to accept rather than hard to understand. It is that astounding claim of Jesus that 'unless we eat of, feed on, the flesh of the Son of Man' we have no life in him.[17] This flesh is 'true food'; it is the bread that came down from heaven; 'whoever feeds on this bread will live for ever'. It is a picture of the Lord Jesus himself as 'living bread', 'if anyone eats of this bread, he will live for ever'. This bread, given for the life of the world is his flesh. In other words, the emphasis in this passage is that we are to 'feed on' Jesus himself. It has been pointed out that there are two distinct words in this passage in the original which have different shades of meaning, although both are translated as 'feed' or 'eat' in most English versions. The first word for 'feed', meaning to consume or devour, comes several times in John chapter 6 (up to verse 54). Then, comes a different, stronger word meaning to chew, munch or gnaw. This word seems to stress, as with physical chewing, a slow but constant process.

So, what does this mean? How, and in what respects are we to feed, gnaw, munch on Jesus? Well, just as physical food becomes part of us, so too spiritually does Christ. Part of us, one with us. As bread makes life possible so Christ makes spiritual life possible – he 'came down from heaven to give life to the world'. It is by faith that we are personally to accept, appropriate and assimilate, spiritually digest all that Jesus is and has done for us by his death upon the cross and by his resurrection and ascension to the right hand of the Father. The words of the Anglican prayer book explain this succinctly – we are 'to feed on him in our hearts by faith with thanksgiving'. It is Christ himself who is the real spiritual food, the only source of our spiritual life and growth. We are sustained by the life that is found only in Jesus.

---

17 John 6:51-58

How does this relate to what has been said above about eating, feasts and communion? Eating good meals take time, they are not to be hurried, they are, hopefully times of relaxation and include conversation and listening to others. This is part of what it means to 'feed on' Christ. Spending time with him, relaxing with him, talking to him in prayer and above all listening to what he has to say to us. He comes to 'eat with us and we with him'.[18] And, as at the end of a meal we should be satisfied, replete; so it is with feeding on Christ.

The other means of spiritual feeding, clearly related to the above, is through God's word the bible. This God given food is described as attractive, sweeter than honey in the comb,[19] hidden manna,[20] good and delightful,[21] satisfying[22] and comforting in affliction.[23] It is to be savoured, rejoiced in[24] and 'stored up'.[25] Isaiah recounts the blessings, the richness of the provision, that result from eating this 'bread'. It is available, free (given), and sustains the true life of the soul, embracing every need. We are to delight in God's word, like Jeremiah;[26] it became to him a joy, despite the sadness of the situation he was in at the time. This was Ezekiel's experience too; in his vision[27] he was commanded to eat the scroll upon which God's words were written, he was to 'fill his stomach' with it and, when it had yet to enter his stomach, he found it 'sweet to the taste'. He had to masticate the scroll, to make the message his own; his stomach was so full there was no room for his own words. God's word then was taken into his

---

18 Revelation 3:20
19 Psalm 19:10; 119:103
20 Revelation 2:17
21 Psalm 119: 14, 16, 24, 92: Isaiah 55:2
22 Proverbs 13:25
23 Psalm 119:48
24 Psalm 119:162
25 Psalm 119:11,27,48; Isaiah 55:1,2
26 Jeremiah 15:16
27 Ezekiel 2:8-10; 3:1-3

very being. Again, this too was the command of the voice from heaven to John in his vision described in Revelation chapter 10. He was to ask the angel for the scroll, to take it and then eat it. As with Ezekiel it was sweet to the taste, like honey, but once in the stomach it turned bitter. As with Ezekiel, this was a hard message God had given him.

Just as there are different kinds of physical food so it is with God's word. Both the author of Hebrews and Paul[28] distinguish between spiritual milk and 'strong' meat. Peter, writing to young Christians (new born babes) urges them to have an appetite for the 'pure spiritual milk' of God's word.[29] The implication here is that milk is for those who have not grown in the Christian life and who are not ready for anything stronger. Milk in this sense means the basic teachings of the bible, the elementary teachings about Christ.[30] However, to really grow demands solid food; they will never go on to maturity, never advance on a diet simply of milk; they were behaving like babies. The lapse of time did not bring spiritual maturity. One wonders how these criticisms might apply to today's church.

Of course, milk is not only for babies! It is not only nutritious but refreshing! After living in Nigeria for several years, and where there was no fresh milk available, the first thing we did when we reached an European airport was to drink a glass of cold, creamy and refreshing milk! A good idea, even for mature believers, is to return frequently to the basics of the faith and to ponder anew the wonder of Christ's death and resurrection and, in Paul's words to 'keep in memory' these great facts.[31]

But what about the 'strong meat', the 'solid food'? What is this? We need to go on and take in, consume the more difficult parts of God's word; it is the whole of God's word that is our spiritual

28 1 Corinthians 3:2
29 1 Peter 2:2
30 Hebrews 5:12-14
31 1 Corinthians 15: 1-8

food. What these passages teach is that we are to grow in likeness to Jesus, to be able to 'discriminate between what is good and bad' and to effectively teach others so as to enable them to grasp spiritual truth.

In summary then let us take the different aspects involved in eating (invitation, preparation, digestion, absorption) and relate them to spiritual feeding. First then there is the invitation; we are to 'come' to God's word with excitement and anticipation; the Lord really wants to speak to us through it. Then we are to 'take', to respond. However, even before this preparation is involved, just as the body is being prepared to accept and eat the food waiting on the table. The spiritual preparation is prayer that we would hear God's voice individually through what we read. We do this in the silence and in wonder. We ask for help to understand, to be taught by it and have the wisdom to apply what is said to our everyday lives. 'Open Thou thy word that we may behold wonderful things from it'.[32] Then, just as we have regular times for physical food so too it is good to have set times for our spiritual daily bread. Of course, this will vary with each individual but it is certainly good to take something from God's word with us to think around, to 'digest' during the working day. It is this digestive process that is the most important of all and, like physical digestion, this takes time. It needs to be absorbed, to be taken in, to become part of us and to make a difference to the way we live. The result of this 'eating' is growth both in grace and in the knowledge of the Lord. We then find increasingly that God's word, like good physical food, is enjoyable and satisfying, a 'delight'!

---

32   Psalm 119:18

6 DRINKING

'If any man thirst let him come to me and drink'[1]

To drink means to swallow a liquid beverage (in the bible, water, wine, milk) or figuratively, it means to eagerly accept or take in, especially that which refreshes and nourishes our spiritual lives. In contrast, to thirst, the sensation caused by a need to drink, is to desire, to long for, to crave. This is true both physically and spiritually; for both, drinking is essential for life.

We are composed mainly of water; 75% by weight in infancy and about 55% in old age. This water is both inside cells (the intracellular space, where most of the body's water resides) and outside cells (extracellular water) as, for example blood and cerebrospinal fluid. Water is the most important dietary component; without it we would die. It is possible to tolerate thirty to forty days without solid food with no apparent ill effects depending on the climate, but survival time is much shorter if water is unavailable; perhaps only three days when the climate is hot.

We obtain water not only by fluid intake, about a litre a day, but also from food since all foods contain water. Indeed, some fruits are about 80% water. The other source of our body water comes from oxidation processes in our cells; perhaps as much as 0.5 litre a day comes from this source. This is small in relation to the human need for water (about 2-2.5 litres a day) but some animals, like the desert rat, can exist almost indefinitely on cellular oxidation processes as their source of water.

The amount of fluid in the body remains largely constant and is in a dynamic steady state; this is known as the water balance and is controlled by a part of the brain called the hypothalamus. This balance depends both on water intake and on the amount

1   John 7: 37

excreted from the body in urine, faeces, through the lungs (about 0.5 litre is expired daily in the expired air) and through the skin, especially through sweating particularly in a hot dry environment. This water loss from our non-waterproof skin, could be up to several litres each hour as part of attempts to control body temperature. Usually however it is about 2-2.5 litres a day. It is not possible to limit water excretion beyond about half this amount; the minimum urine output is about 0.5 litres/day. From this it is clear that survival with no water intake in only possible for a few days.

Thirst is a sensation resulting from the need to drink. This desire is strong, a craving. It occurs when body fluids are depleted by as little as 2%; for a normal 70kg person this means as little as 100ml. At double this deficit the mouth and throat feel dry whilst above this level the tongue swells, speech becomes difficult and there may be apathy and sleepiness. Above 10% water deprivation (a loss of water to the body of about five litres) the subject needs rapid assistance. The lethal limit is 20% of normal body water volume. It is easy for infants to become dehydrated through giving concentrated fruit drinks because, with such hypertonic solutions, they need more water to remove the solute especially if this is common salt. This sensation of thirst is not simply due to having a dry mouth (otherwise it could be relieved by a mouthful of water) but is due to changes in the chemical composition of the blood. This is registered (metered) within the brain at a kind of 'drinking centre'. Thirst during illness is a consequence of increased water loss through sweating, in an attempt to lower the increased body temperature, and through vomiting and diarrhoea.

The reason for death due to dehydration, for example at sea in an open boat especially under hot conditions (refugees attempting to cross the Mediterranean to reach Europe) is the increased bodily concentrations of salt, protein and it's main, and toxic, breakdown product urea. It is vital that these are removed from the body.

As one would expect from the above there are many references to the importance of drinking water in scripture. This essential need for water is illustrated in the conflict about the ownership of wells in Old Testament times. For example, the quarrels between the herdsmen of Terah and Isaac; 'the water is ours'.[2] Then it was at a well outside the city of Nahor in Mesopotamia that Abraham's servant met Rebekah.[3] The Lord supplied Samson with water from a 'hollow place' after Samson had 'struck' a thousand men and was, understandably, thirsty as a result; indeed he was so thirsty that he called upon the Lord saying 'I shall die of thirst'.[4] Another prayer for physical water was answered when Moses struck a rock at Horeth in the wilderness, 'why did you bring us out of Egypt to kill us with thirst; give us water to drink'[5]. This water was provided by God.

These instances illustrate the essential importance of a God-given provision of physical water, without which we would die. But figuratively, there is our desperate need for spiritual water; this basic spiritual need too is met by God. There is the reiterated promise that God would provide 'water in the desert', the 'desert' illustrating the place of our basic spiritual needs. God promises to 'open rivers on the bare mountain heights' and to provide pools of water to those whose spiritual tongues are parched with thirst.[6] This gift is an abundant one ('I will pour water')[7], a pouring not simply a sprinkling.

In the wonderful account of the meeting of Jesus with the 'woman at the well'[8] outside the town of Sychar (a well originating from the time of Jacob) Jesus speaks of being able to meet our spiritual thirst with his 'living water'.[9] This 'living water' is

---

2   Genesis 26:17- 22

3   Genesis 24:10–14

4   Judges 15:15-19

5   Exodus 17:6

6   Isaiah 41:17,18

7   Isaiah 44:3

8   John 4:5,6

9   John 4:14

spiritual life from Jesus himself; it is likened to a 'spring of water welling up to eternal life', cool, refreshing and inexhaustible. Jesus first requests literal water from the well because he was tired and thirsty; however, what he gave in return was spiritual water. This water is essential for our spiritual life; it is frequently needed (not just once) and is freely available ('without price'),[10] to anyone who believes in him. This 'water of life'[11] strengthens, refreshes and nourishes the soul.[12] Spiritual thirst is quenched and satisfied.[13] As Augustine of Hippo said 'God has put salt in our mouths so that we might thirst for him'. Indeed, our souls do thirst for God[14] and the life-giving water to quench that thirst comes only from God himself.[15]

That great cry ('aloud') of Jesus in John 7[16] 'if anyone thirst let him come to me and drink' came during that part of the daily ritual of the Feast of Tabernacles when water, taken from the Pool of Siloam, was literally 'poured out' from a golden pitcher. This 'pouring out' took place on each of the eight days of the Feast except the last. It was on this last day of the Feast, the 'great day' of the Festival kept as a Sabbath, that Jesus made this great declaration, pointing to himself as the one in whom spiritual thirst could be assuaged. Jesus then made the stupendous claim that 'if anyone thirst let him come to me and drink';[16] we slake our spiritual thirst only at this spring. Only Jesus satisfies. We derive our spiritual lives from Christ. All we have to do is simply to 'come'[17] believing who he is and accepting what he has done for us in mediating God's salvation.

---

10 Revelation 22:17

11 Revelation 21:6

12 John 7:37

13 Matthew 5:6

14 Psalms 42:2, 63:1, 107:5, 143:6

15 Psalm 105:41; Ezekiel 47:1,12; Zechariah 13:1,14:8; Joel 3:18

16 John 7:37-39

17 Revelation 22:17; Isaiah 55:1

There is a sense that when we receive this gift of the 'water of life' we become the source of that same gift to others. 'Where the Spirit is,' wrote William Temple, 'He flows forth; if there is no flowing forth then He is not there'. So, this 'living water' of which Jesus speaks, this life-giving Holy Spirit who comes to all who accept Jesus, becomes a source of spiritual refreshment not only for ourselves but also for others.

Wine

'The most hygienic of beverages' said Pasteur. A mixture of wine and water[18] when drunk by soldiers during the North Africa Campaign of WW2, resulted in them having fewer gastrointestinal diseases. And, when water was scarce the addition of wine made supplies of water last longer. Hippocrates (of the medical 'oath') argued that wine drunk with an equal quantity of water relieves anxiety whilst Galen, the 'father of modern medicine' recommended for fatigue a mixture of wine, honey and water. Perhaps this was the reason that wine was offered by Boaz to his workers in the field, including Ruth.[19] One possible reason for this positive effect in reducing fatigue is the high level of potassium, a beneficial effect quite independent of the alcohol content.

The medical qualities of wine were recognised by the apostle Paul, who recommended a 'little wine for the stomach' for the young Timothy,[20] whose intestinal problem perhaps resulted from drinking contaminated water which could have led to dysentery. Understandable and good advice then. But what are we to make of the next phrase in this verse, 'and for your frequent ailments'. What were these I wonder? And, how were these alleviated by drinking wine?

There is a long history of the antibiotic properties of some wines. The Good Samaritan in the Jesus parable, retold by doctor

18   The mingled wine of Proverbs 9:2,5
19   Ruth 2:14 (ESV)
20   1 Timothy 5:23

Luke, bound up the wounds of the half-dead traveller who fell among thieves with a mixture of oil and wine.[21] This antibiotic property of wine has been linked with anthocyanins which are present in wine, but not in fresh grape juice. It is said to be more active against some microorganisms than penicillin. The most efficacious antimicrobial effect apparently comes from grapes left to rot on the vine in the presence of fungi, to produce sweet desert wines such as the Hungarian 'Tokai'. One of my former colleagues, Professor Jean-Claude Stoclet in Strasburg, worked for some time on the chemical substances responsible for the cardioprotective effects of red wine, which forms part of the so-called healthy 'Mediterranean diet'. For those interested there is a reasonable summary of these protective effects of wine in a book by Roger Corder.

The importance of wine in Jewish social customs is well illustrated in Jesus' first miracle when he turned water into 'good wine', the 'best until last'.[22] This incident symbolises wine as a gift to 'gladden man's heart'[23] and illustrates the joy and fellowship of a happy occasion. 'Wine is for drinking, water is for washing and milk is for children'!

Although 'everything created by God is good', scripture quite clearly condemns the immoderate use of wine and the resultant drunkenness and inebriation. 'Wine is a mocker, whoever is led astray by it is not wise'.[24] Continued use leads to forgetfulness[25] with long term effects on brain function. There is a description in the Talmud of the woman who consumes too much wine; 'one glass of wine makes a woman pretty, two makes her hateful, three makes her lust invitingly'. We leave for the imagination what the

---

21 Luke10:34
22 John 2:1-10
23 Psalm 104:15, Ruth 3:7
24 Proverbs 20:1; 23:20,21
25 Proverbs 31:4-6

fourth glass leads to! It may provoke the desire ('aflame')[26] 'but it takes away from the performance'.[27] The examples of Noah and Lot are condemned[28] and Nabal[29] died, probably from cardiac failure, after a drunken feast in his house, an example perhaps of 'binge drinking'. The command then is 'be not drunk with wine'[30] and even moderate drinking is wrong if it makes another stumble in the faith.[31] Total abstinence may be recommended but never be enforced as a Christian obligation.

The wine-vinegar as offered to Christ on the Cross was soured wine. Jesus took it[32] not to ease the pain or diminish his response to pain but to moisten his throat to enable him to make that great cry[33] from the Cross 'it is finished'.[34] Salvation completed!

---

26 Isaiah 5:11

27 Shakespeare's Macbeth 11.30

28 Genesis 9: 20,21; 19: 33–35

29 1 Samuel 25:36-38

30 1 Corinthians 5:11; Ephesians 5: 18; Titus 1:7

31 Romans 14:20,21

32 John 19:29,30

33 Matthew 27:50; Mark 15:37

34 John 19:30

7 SLEEPING
'A little sleep, a little slumber'[1]

We begin with a definition! Sleep is a state of reduced awareness and activity that occurs at regular intervals, usually daily; if it happens seasonally it is hibernation. It is then 'reduced awareness', not complete cessation of bodily activity. That is death. As the author of the Song of Solomon puts it 'I was asleep but my heart was awake'.[2] Just as well! And not just the heart, some muscles, though not all, are relaxed, body temperature is maintained and the intestines and the liver are still dealing with the evening meal. There is also increased activity in certain areas of the brain, especially those parts that deal with the processing of information gained during the waking hours although, of course, there is also a suspension of mental activity ('a dark slice out of time') in other parts of the brain.

One area of the brain, the hypothalamus (which is where the 'sleep switch' is situated) is particularly concerned with physiological changes during sleep; the shift from consciousness of the outer world to the almost complete 'sensory blindness' and decreased responsiveness to external stimuli. This 'sleep switch' is influenced by temperature (the hot baths that cause drowsiness) and by the (circadian) rhythms active, for example, when moving from one time zone to another. Lesions to this part of the brain, for example those resulting from 'sleeping sickness' (*encephalitis lethargica*), lead to prolonged periods of sleep.

Those parts of the brain which deal with 'housekeeping chores' (repairing cellular metabolic damage, strengthening important neural networks and connections between cells) show increased metabolic activity during sleep. These include those processes

---

1 Proverbs 6:10
2 Song of Solomon 5:2

involved in effective learning, and the formation of memories from information gleaned when we are awake. So, sleep after learning is critical to the learning processes. To 'sleep on it' is good advice! There is also some evidence that fresh mental insights, those 'good ideas', that breakthrough thinking, occur during sleep. We know of those experiences of waking during the night with that splendid solution for a problem which we have been puzzling over during the previous day. One wonders what such 'eureka moments' have been responsible for! Great music? Certainly, Otto Loewi, the scientist responsible for the concept, in the heart, that chemical messengers are released from autonomic nerves that then modify that activity of cardiac muscle cells, is said to have come up with the idea, confirmed experimentally, after waking from sleep. Mulling over problems before going to bed and then sleeping on them, providing one can drift off to sleep in the first place, may provide an answer in the morning. Or, that idea for next Sunday's sermon? Good to have a bedside pencil and notebook handy just in case!

Although we spend perhaps 30% of our lives sleeping, more than this in childhood and usually less in old age, we still know relatively little about why we sleep. What precisely is the function? Now in my eighties, I have probably been asleep for 25-30 years. Was this time wasted? No, sleep is vitally necessary; sleep loss is disabling. Attempts to 'steal' time, by reducing sleep in order to work, is self-destructive. Prolonged sleep deprivation leads to amnesia, memory lapses, a reduced ability to concentrate and performance impairment. Drowsiness whilst driving increases markedly (four-fold) the risk of collision and is responsible for hundreds of accidents each year. This is on a par with elevated blood levels of alcohol and of some drugs. Sleep deprivation also leads to an increase in appetite, to weight gain due to the deposition of fat, and a reduced insulin response to glucose – changes characteristic of the ageing process.

Short daytime naps are seen in Japan as an acceptable part of the working day with publicly available street-side 'sleeping capsules'. Taking a nap of say five to ten minutes, could turn out to be an important weapon in the battle against coronary morbidity. A brief recent newspaper article from a place of learning in Hertfordshire suggests that people could become happier if they took short naps (less than 30 minutes) during the day – 'nappiness'. Many questions! Who was persuaded to fund such a study? How was this happiness defined? Jesus indeed turned the way of looking at happiness upside down;[3] one that could survive disappointment and suffering, based not on outward circumstances but on inner character (serenity, 'blessed') that by its very nature (joyful acceptance, humble gratitude) could not be taken away. Or, to quote Shakespeare, 'sleep knits up the sleeve of care'.

Why then do we sleep? 'A biological dilemma of the first order' and yet it is more critical for health than heredity, exercise or diet. Well, essentially it is to enable repairs, restoration to occur resulting from the metabolic damage resulting from wakefulness; it is to consolidate the tasks crucial for improving performance, to review neural connections and hormonal secretion (for example, those that regulate growth), to foster 'breakthrough thinking' and to maintain those 'housekeeping chores' essential for critical mental functions.

Let us summarise what God's word says about sleep.

1. Sleep is a Gift from God

'God grants (gives) sleep to those He loves'.[4] In the Scriptures it is therefore no surprise to learn that sleep is referred to as a gift from God.[5] 'I lay myself down and sleep; I wake again, for the Lord sustains me. I stretch myself out. I sleep and then I'm up again, rested, tall and steady'.[6] This was sleep that was clearly restorative and refreshing. The likely background to this psalm is

---

3 Matthew 5:3–11
4 Psalm 127:2
5 Psalm 4:8
6 Psalm 3:5,6

of particular interest. David was fleeing for his life following his son's Absalom's revolt. He had little time, the enemy was already entering the city of Jerusalem. David and his entourage, slowed by the presence of women and children, eventually, after a hard day's trek, reached the Transjordan sheep lands that he knew so well from his earlier days.[7] Exhausted, he puts his shield over himself and sleeps.[8] In this kind of situation most of us would have turned over the events of the day. For David, if he did that, there would be thoughts about the surprising strength of the revolt, the discouragement of his meeting with Shimei,[9] the nearness of his pursuers, and the calls of those who said that God must have abandoned him.[10] Yet God gave him this wonderful gift of sleep, renewing him and preparing him for the further trek next day to safety. That sleep was exactly the right answer to David's need. I wonder if David had asked God for a good night of sleep? If so that prayer was answered. If not, God gave it anyway, a miracle of divine working. This was the 'sweet sleep' of Proverbs 3:24!

There is then a place for resting and for 'putting the conflict on one side'. This is part of God's grace; His order for us is daylight for work, night for sleep.[11] The New Testament equivalent would be Romans 8:28 and Matthew 6:33, for peaceful sleep is the opposite of anxiety. God made sleep as a continual daily reminder that we should not be anxious but should rest and trust in Him. We are to rejoice in the gift of sleep as a symptom not of indolence, or even of sorrow[12] but of trust in our Heavenly Father. And, after we fall asleep and rest[13]

---

7   1 Samuel 23:14
8   Psalm 3:3
9   2 Samuel 16:5-8
10   Psalm 3:1,2
11   Psalm 104:19-23
12   Luke 22:45
13   Matthew 26:40,43

we recover[14] and work. But, of course, as Eutychus discovered,[15] sleep has dangers. Just as well that today's churches are seldom on the third floor, especially when the sermons are long!

2. God does not Sleep, 'God is up all Night'!

God 'neither slumbers nor sleeps'.[16] He is a tireless worker. When God 'caused a deep sleep to fall on Adam' he continued working. He made woman. What a wonderful piece of work! One of the great truths of this Psalm is God 'helping', 'protecting', 'keeping' as we sleep just as when we are awake. We need sleep. God knows that. God understands that; and when his Son Jesus came to earth he too needed sleep.[17] But God himself does not need it. He is always awake, always working, always helping, always protecting. He 'neither slumbers nor sleeps'.[18] God is a tireless worker, His protection is comprehensive, day and night, coming and going, now and for ever. We are, as Timothy Dudley-Smith wrote, 'safe in the shadow of the Lord by darkness as by day'.

3. Sleep as Death

Sleep is also used in Scripture as a metaphor for death. This is presumably because of the similarity in appearance between a sleeping person and a dead body; both are characterised by restfulness and peace. This picture suggests the sleeper does not cease to exist whilst the body 'sleeps' in death; the dead person continues to exist despite the fact that he can no longer communicate with those around him. The reason the bible speaks this way is in order to make more intelligible something that is beyond our present comprehension. In the Old Testament for example the phrase 'slept with his fathers' comes many times in the books of Samuel, Kings and Chronicles. Jeremiah speaks of death as 'perpetual sleep',

---

14 Matthew 26: 45,46
15 Acts 20:9
16 Psalm 121:3
17 Luke 8:23
18 Psalm 121:4

sleeping in the company of many[19] and the psalmist asks God to 'consider and answer' him lest he 'sleep the sleep of death'.[20]

In the New Testament the same word (katheudo) is used of natural sleep and, in some places, also of the death of the body, for example of Lazarus[21] and of the daughter of Jairus.[22] The same word is also used of indifference, insensitivity, to spiritual things by believers.[23]

We have already seen (above) that during normal sleep parts of the body are still active such as the lungs, muscles and heart; 'I sleep but my heart is awake'.[24] In the sleep of death our physical heart may have stopped but our 'spiritual heart' continues. Our breathing may have ceased but the breath of the Spirit remains. Our muscles (prior to rigor mortis) may be flaccid but our 'spiritual muscles' grow whilst we sleep. In his 2004 Didsbury lectures Stephen Smalley emphasises that 'spiritual sleep, even more than the physical must involve growth as well as life'. And, as in normal sleep, we are not inactive. In Revelation[25] the resting saints are clearly conscious; they ask about justice (6:10) and have a vibrant hope of 'waking up' to resurrection life.

We move at death from the dimension of time and space to that of eternity where our personalities are not 'cut off' but differently expressed. We remain recognisable not by our physical characteristics but rather by our inner personalities; it is an intermediate state between physical death and the bodily resurrection. There is no loss of individual identity. And if being asleep in the Lord is being 'with Him', is 'far better'[26] and is being 'at home'[27] then this implies a quite new quality of existence. We

---

19   Jeremiah 51:39, 57
20   Psalm 13:3
21   John 11:11
22   Matthew 9:24; Mark 5: 39; Luke 8:52
23   Ephesians 5:14
24   Song of Solomon 5:2
25   Revelation 6:9-11
26   Philippians 1:23
27   2 Corinthians 5:6-9

sleep in death, as in normal life, to awake still, as always and at once, in the presence of Jesus. In death, as in this present life, we are in the hands of our loving God.

4. Sleeplessness

Sleep problems are common, particularly in children and in the elderly. In Scotland, according to the BBC radio programme 'Call Kay', one in three people have difficulty in sleeping and in the United States one study found that only 5% of people were reported as never having trouble sleeping. Why is this?

There are two particular examples of sleeplessness in the Old Testament that may provide a partial answer. The first is in the book of Esther. Ahasuerus, the king, had a particular difficulty in sleeping[28] after he had given an order, influenced by Haman, that all Jews in his vast country should be annihilated.[29] However, because God is on the throne, it is the Jewish Queen Esther who is present 'for such a time as this'. She invites the king, and Haman, to a banquet and it is after this that Ahasuerus had difficulty in sleeping. Why was this? Did he have too much to drink? He clearly had an impressive wine cellar, he served from this liberally to his guests, drinking from a variety of golden goblets[30] and the wine came from a variety of different sources (the phrase 'the king instructed the wine stewards to serve each man what he wished' seems to imply this). Although alcohol can induce sleep (it is after all a central nervous system depressant) some of the breakdown products have the opposite effect, which partially explains periods of wakefulness several hours after alcohol ingestion (there were certainly times of 'high spirits'). Or, he may have needed to pass urine after excessive fluid intake. Was he in pain, too cold, too hot, or did he have financial worries with the expense of all those banquets? More likely perhaps he was intrigued by Queen Esther's request that he and Haman come to two successive banquets

---

28 Esther 6:1
29 Esther 3:12,13
30 Esther 1:7

before she was willing to respond to his question 'what is your request'.[31] Maybe he was puzzling over what that request might be.

The other Old Testament example of sleeplessness comes in the book of Daniel. King Darius, having ordered Daniel to be put into the lion's den,[32] could not sleep; as the AV puts it 'sleep fled from him'. It seems that Darius was concerned about Daniel's safety. He got up early next morning to see if God had been able to rescue His servant. He could hardly wait to see what had happened; he 'got up at the first light of dawn' and 'hurried', he 'called from a distance'. So, concern, anxiety to see what was happening, kept him from sleeping. Or, had he exercised too close to bedtime, drunk too much coffee or forgotten his Horlicks? Concern for others, or for oneself, and worry, can be added to the physical factors (temperature, light and dark, noise, different surroundings) that can keep us from sleeping.

So, what can we do about sleeplessness? And, if we wake up in the early hours what should we do? Does God wake us sometimes, when we would normally be asleep, for a purpose? Is it for worship? Psalm 92 speaks about 'proclaiming (to God) about His love and faithfulness at night'. Could it be that we have been woken to pray, God prompting us to pray for someone at a time when that person is in danger? My own solution for dealing with these 'wake up times' is to pray for those folk I had prayed for during the previous day. For example, if I awake in the middle of a Thursday night I would go over all those various Hungarian friends I have prayed for during the day (Thursday being my 'Hungarian' prayer day). We are certainly to make effective use of those waking up times.

But what else can we do about sleeplessness? The East Dunbartonshire Council booklet on 'sleep problems' recommends eating lettuce last thing at night (quite a yawn!). One suggestion, which seems to have been the answer to King Ahasuerus 'sleep problem', is to get out of bed, sit somewhere quiet with a pen and

31 Esther 5:8
32 Daniel 6:16-20

paper, read, or listen to music (but not too loud). Ahasuerus, being a king, got someone else to read to him[33] stories that were mainly about himself and his exploits. What he chose was not especially exciting but very relevant to his present situation. Nothing more sleep-inducing than to hear stories about yourself!

---

33   Esther 6:1,2

8 DREAMING

'We are like them that dream'[1]

Once again, we start with a definition. Dreaming is an active mental state associated with sleep, 'commonplace unilateral impressions which enter the mind without external help', recollections, the 'memory of the senses'. Jean Anthelme Brillat-Savarin, who, in 1825 in his delightful and amusing meditations on taste, food and good living, talked about 'the four faculties' (sight, hearing, touch, memory) which are usually watching over and connecting the one with the other, but which in dreaming are 'left to their own devices'! So, we plunge into the 'dream world' when the brain is no longer 'tied down', not restricted by messages from the outside world and starts to 'free wheel'. And it is commonplace; we all dream, and any impressions to the contrary are rooted in poor recall, our inability to remember.

When do we dream? More often in childhood, when dreams are of games, gardens and cheerful things, and especially in the first year of life, during which time about half of our total sleep pattern occurs when electrical brain activity is similar to that during wakefulness; this is called 'rapid eye movement or REM sleep'. We dream much less (about 20% of total sleep time) in old age although, in scripture[2] it is the 'old men who dream dreams'. Such dreams are often about past pleasures, old friends long since dead, business, travel and money.

In mid-life we spend about one to two hours per night in the REM phase of sleep which means so we spend about 25% of our lives dreaming – a lifetime of about 200,000 dreams! But how many can we remember? It is those of childhood that are remembered best in later life. My wife, as a child in wartime Britain and with

---

1 Psalm 126:1
2 Joel 2:28; Acts 2:17

her father in the navy, had a dream in which she felt she was falling (said to be a sign of insecurity) but landed with both feet on the bible! Standing on the promises of God even at that young age! Apparently, men dream more about work, possible redundancy and financial security whilst those of women, whose dreams last longer, are more about the home and family members. We tend to dream most at either end of our sleeping time, the first half of the night, when dreams seem to be more related to reality, and especially towards morning, when the dreams are quite emotionally intense, bizarre and more easily remembered.

But why do we dream at all? Are they glimpses of the past or future or simply random cerebral junk? Or is it the brain doing its filing, the offline brain doing housekeeping and reworking, reappraising, the events and issues of the previous day, storing and cross-referencing? Scientists (including myself) and others have testified that the sudden solution to a problem has come during sleep. A notebook handy at the bedside in case that good idea has been forgotten by morning! But was that 'solution' really a dream?

Scripture is full of examples of people dreaming and these are mostly found in the Old Testament. Abraham dreamt, Jacob dreamt, as did Joseph, Ezekiel and Daniel. But so did Pharaoh (and his servants) and Nebuchadnezzar. These were all visions in sleep. Most of these dreams, such as those of Jacob, Pharaoh and Pharaoh's servants, required interpretation.

There are fewer examples in the New Testament but when they do occur they are dreams of revelation, knowledge, protection, direction or illumination. Some of these are clearly related to everyday events whereas others are quite unrelated to what had happened previously. In Matthew's gospel, when Joseph discovered that Mary his betrothed, was pregnant by the Holy Spirit, he resolved to divorce her quietly. As he was thinking about this, as he 'considered these things', 'an angel of the Lord appeared to him in a dream' with instructions from

God – 'do not fear to take Mary as your wife'.[3] Later, once again 'an angel of the Lord appeared to Joseph in a dream' with the warning to leave for Egypt and avoid Herod's planned execution. This was then a dream of warning and protection as well as of instruction.

Even later, whilst still in Egypt, the same dream re-occurred, with the instruction to return to Israel. This too was a dream of knowledge ('Herod is dead') and of direction ('arise and go'). After this, Joseph was warned, again in a dream, not to go to Judah but instead to leave for Galilee. In summary then, these dreams, which were from the Lord, were of discovery, assurance, protection, warning, direction and guidance. And in all these instances Joseph obeyed.

There are of course many instances, other than by dreams, where we are simply told that God 'revealed' ('uncovered') something by His Spirit. For example, we are told that that 'it had been revealed to him' (Simeon) by the Holy Spirit that he would not die until he had seen the Christ child.[4] Because this revelation came as he entered the Temple precincts 'in the Spirit', this was clearly not a dream; it was a waking revelation.

The other significant events are in Acts. In chapter 10 Peter, hungry and presumably thirsty (dehydrated through exposure to the heat of the sun) and at the normal time of prayer, falls into a trance (Greek ekstasis). This is a condition in which consciousness, the perception of natural circumstances, is withheld and the normal action of the senses suspended. Only mad dogs and Englishmen go out in the midday sun! Some authors have seen this as Peter, weary from his wayfaring, falling asleep at prayer (not an unusual experience for some), with the last impression of his tired drowsy mind being the sight of a ship at sail (the same word as 'awning' in verse 11). Certainly, tiredness, hunger and thirst, heat and perhaps the smell of the tannery in his nostrils,

---

3 Matthew 1:19, 20
4 Luke 2:26

would predispose to sleep and the imagery of food. Whether this was dreaming, daydreaming, vision or trance it was clearly God speaking.

It was a dream with historic consequences, the opening of the church to non-Jews. God was 'working from both ends', speaking both to Cornelius and leading him 'by the nose' to Peter's domicile in the tannery.[5] Peter himself needed the assurance that it was God who was speaking; note the 'three times' in verse 16, perhaps a gentle reminder from the Lord both of his threefold denial and his subsequent re-commission. Certainly Peter could at last say 'now I understand' because there follows, in his subsequent proclamation of the gospel, one of the clearest declarations in Acts of the apostolic message, the kerygma.

The question arises as to whether there is distinction between revelation by dreams and by vision? My former minister Dr JGSS Thomson, in his article for the first edition of the *New Bible Dictionary*[6] concluded that 'the border line between vision, dream or trance is difficult, if not impossible to determine' but that 'all essentially involve a special awareness of God and of His willingness to reveal Himself and communicate with man'. He really wants to speak with us. And, as far as dreams and visions are concerned, in the New Testament especially, they occurred at special times in history; the incarnation, the spread of the gospel to gentiles and the entry of the Good News into Europe.[7] The other important point is that these, largely nocturnal, events, whether dreams or visions, were remembered on waking and acted upon.[8]

Note that God speaks in this way to unbelievers as well as to believers. Thus, in the Old Testament God spoke in dreams to

---

5   Acts 10:3-7
6   The Inter-Varsity Fellowship, London, 1962, page 323.
7   Acts 16:9
8   Acts 16:10

Laban,[9] Pharaoh[10] and to Pharaoh's servants.[11] Nebuchadnezzar, whose dreams interrupted his sleep and which made him afraid[12] needed an interpretation and this was revealed, also in a dream, a 'night vision', to Daniel.[13]

The Hebrew noun (*chalom*) is used both for ordinary dreams during sleep[14] and to prophetic dreams and visions, 'a prophet or a dreamer or dreams';[15] that is dreams as a means of revelation. Most of the examples are in Genesis. Abimelech's was a warning dream ('do not take')[16] whereas Jacob's 'ladder dream'[17] was a dream of promise, that God would always be with him not only at the onset of his journey but again later, 'here I am', God said to me in a dream.[18] These were dreams both of assurance and instruction ('arise, go, return'). In contrast, Joseph's irrepressible dreams were prophetic, they foretold what would happen years later; they were portents of what God would do.[19]

It is interesting that the dreams of unbelievers need to be interpreted by those who were in touch with the living God and who needed God to shed meaning on them. This was a special God-given gift. Joseph, in his interpretation of the dreams of Pharaoh's servants, acknowledged 'I cannot interpret your dream but God can'.[20] He clearly had this unique gift from God but did not boast of this skill or seek to draw attention to himself. Solomon's dream[21] is interesting in that it was a

9   Genesis 31:24
10   Genesis 41:1
11   Genesis 40:5
12   Daniel 2:3; 4:4,5
13   Daniel 2:19
14   Job 7:14
15   Deuteronomy 13
16   Genesis 20:3
17   Genesis 28:11-15
18   Genesis 31:11,13
19   Genesis 37:5,9
20   Genesis 41:15,16
21   1 Kings 3:5,6,11

two-way conversation with God and led to urgent prayer and worship; still in a dream!

Does God still 'speak' through dreams? Many African believers, especially from a Muslim background, have testified to the fact that God has spoken to them in this way and spoken especially of Jesus. Indeed, some African indigenous churches seem to have been started by a dream without any outside contact with bearers of the gospel message. The Nigerian theologian Tokunboh Adeyemo, the editor of the African Bible Commentary, has noted two tests to determine whether these dream messages are truly from God. After all, like other gifts from God, they can be abused. First, any dream that contradicts Scripture is not of God.[22] Second, Spirit-filled believers are able to differentiate between 'real' and counterfeit dreams. This itself accords with Scripture. For example, Jeremiah was able to distinguish the true from the false; the (false) prophets said 'I have dreamed, I have dreamed' and yet made God's people forget his name.[23]

Whilst writing this chapter I received a prayer letter from a friend working in a sensitive part of the world about a man who had been 'seeking' for several years and was getting more and more disillusioned with the system in which he grew up. God used media, conversations over a secure phone line and a dream to bring him to Himself. In the dream he mentioned that Jesus spoke beautiful Urdu!

---

22 See Deuteronomy 13
23 Jeremiah 23:1-40

9 CIRCULATING (BLOOD)
'The life of all flesh is in the blood'[1]
'you have been brought near by the blood of Christ'[2]

The word 'blood' is a noun, a verb, an expletive with myriad meanings and, figuratively, it is a word for passion, temper, emotion and lineage – 'the stuff of kinship'. However, the predominant meaning is 'a bodily humour', a fluid circulating in the blood vessels. It is the 'vital fluid', the 'amiable juice', the bearer of life, or as the King James Bible has it 'the blood is the life thereof'.[3] It is, in the age-old belief, the key to life's deepest secrets, the 'sovereign principle of life', a rich liquid asset and a 'precious deposit'. As William Harvey, the discoverer of the circulation of the blood opined, 'blood lives of itself and depends in no wise upon any part of the body. It is the cause of life in general but also of longer or shorter life; the first to live and the last to die.'[4] It is a warm, sticky, scarlet and soup-like suspension of cells (about 50% of the total volume) in a watery solution (the plasma) containing both electrolytes and non-electrolytes which makes up about 8% of the body weight (5.5 litres in a 70kg man). It is 'a truly remarkable juice'!

In the Old Testament, the word translated blood occurs over 350 times, over two hundred of which refer to death by violence; to shed blood is to commit murder.[5] Blood is synonymous with life, 'the life of the flesh is in the blood'[6]; the high value of life as a gift from God led to the prohibition against eating blood, 'this is a perpetual statute . . . that you eat neither fat nor blood'.[7] Animal blood by the offering

---

1 Leviticus 17:11
2 Ephesians 2:13
3 Leviticus 17:14
4 Keynes, G., *The Life of William Harvey*, Oxford, Clarendon Press, 1978
5 Genesis 9:6
6 Leviticus 17:11
7 Leviticus 3:17

of an animal in substitution, could take the place of sinner's blood in atoning for (covering) sin and these sacrifices prefigure the blood of Christ shed on Calvary, the only truly effective substitutionary atonement. By this shedding, the ebbing away of Jesus' life-blood, we are reconciled to God.[8] We are justified[9] by the blood of his cross.[10]

John's testimony, as a witness of the crucifixion, made note[11] of the fact that the sword thrust into the side of Jesus, 'a careless act by a rough soldier' led to the flowing out of blood and water as a proof that Jesus really did die on the cross. William Temple[12] commented on this 'the evangelist attaches great importance to this strange event, a sign that the Lord, truly dead, is also yet alive'. For Temple, this act is symbolic of the sacrament of Communion (the blood of the new Covenant) and also of baptism (water as a symbol of spiritual life). There is much theological debate as to what this event signifies. Was it, because Jesus was already dead,[13] that the 'water' was the straw-coloured serum, the liquid element of blood? This results within minutes, from the separation of the cellular elements, which form the blood clot (thrombus) from the liquid component (serum) and occurs when blood is withdrawn or spilt. It also happens within the body itself; the formation of 'clots' in blood vessels (thrombosis) takes place especially in veins and when the blood flow is sluggish. This is because the decreased flow permits clotting factors to accumulate instead of being washed away.

Uncontrolled intravascular coagulation is especially likely to occur in static limbs, for example during air travel (deep vein thrombosis; DVT). It is not difficult to visualise that this is likely to occur during crucifixion, because of the fixed static position of the body and the accumulation of blood in the lower limbs, especially

---

8   Romans 5:10
9   Romans 5:9
10 Colossians 1:20
11 John 19:34,35
12 Temple, William, *Readings in St John's Gospel*, London, McMillan, 1961
13 John 19:33

over a six-hour period. This would be accentuated by internal blood loss and by haemoconcentration following the loss of body fluids resulting from sweating in a hot environment; Jesus did after all call out from the cross 'I thirst'.[14]

There is however an alternative explanation. In an interesting article in the Journal of the American Medical Association for March 1986, Dr William Edwards, a pathologist at the Mayo Clinic, gave medical evidence that Jesus was already dead when he was taken down from the cross. His explanation of the 'water and the blood' was that the 'water' was clear pericardial fluid rather than serum. He suggested that the direction of the sword thrust was into the thorax because the word used ('side') is best translated 'pleura'. However, the important thing was not so much how he died but that he really did die on Calvary's Cross. 'Interpretations based on an assumption that Jesus did not die on the cross appear to be at odds with modern medical knowledge'.

What is blood for? I remember one of my granddaughters, after cutting her knee, and as the blood oozed from the wound, asking 'Grandad, what is this blood doing?' A way then of asking what is the function of blood in our bodies? So, what does it 'do'? Well, it has three functions.

First, it has a nutritional function; it provides all that each cell in the body needs for life. This because blood is the medium by which substances are transported around the body. These substances are oxygen (bound to haemoglobin in red cells and in solution), various nutrients (obtained from stores within the body or directly from the gastrointestinal tract), enzymes (from their place of formation) and various other substances, such as hormones (on route to their target organs) and vitamins. Also important is that blood redistributes heat around the body.

Second, blood removes the resultant waste products of cellular metabolism; it cleanses.

Third, it has a protective function against damage and infection.

We consider each of these in turn.

---

14 John 19:28

1. Blood Provides, Nourishes, Feeds

Blood provides all that the cells require to function, to live. Oxygen is carried almost entirely by the red blood cells (erythrocytes) in combination with haemoglobin; this gives blood it's red colour. Nutrients (organic molecules, especially sugars such as glucose, which serve as metabolic fuels), inorganic ions and proteins (which bind hormones) as well as some oxygen, are carried mainly in solution. This requires a system to carry blood to each and every body cell – the cardiovascular system.

This system is comprised of a pump (the heart) and a series of tubes (vessels, about 60,000 miles of them) varying in size from the large, very muscular aorta and main arteries, to the smallest capillaries. These capillaries being fully permeable, allow the exchange of materials to take place from the blood, to and from the cells. The diameter of these capillaries can be so small that some are comparable in size to that of the red blood cells themselves. It is fascinating to watch under the microscope in a living animal (for example, the rich blood supply of the cheek pouch of an anaesthetised hamster) how such cells are able to squeeze through such small vessels. No cell in the body is more than a hairbreadth from such capillary blood.

The American physiologist Alan Burton, introduced his textbook on the physiology and biophysics of the circulation by asking four main questions about the circulation – purpose, priorities, possibilities and problems. He then invited an imaginary group of students (appointed by the Creator) to design such a system; a 'celestial committee for the design of a mammalian circulation'. One factor to be borne in mind was that the amount of blood provided by such a circulation should be in accordance with the individual needs of each group of cells at a particular time. Thus, the heart, responsible for the active propulsion of blood around the body, the brain, the liver (dealing with the breakdown of waste products produced by each cell) and the kidney (responsible for their excretion from the body) would together require about two thirds of the blood output available, about three litres a minute. In contrast, skin and muscle, except during exercise or in a hot environment, and the digestive tract, except after a meal, would require much less. The proportion of the total output of blood by the heart to the various organs of the body is thus capable of being altered to match the demands of those particular physiological (or pathophysiological) circumstances, such as digestion, exercise or weightlessness, occurring at any given time.

What would happen then if this process is interfered with, for example following blood loss through bleeding (haemorrhage) or if the supply of blood is reduced (called ischaemia) which results when a blood vessel is narrowed or completely obstructed? Clearly, because the function of blood is to provide the cells with everything they need to sustain life, it is important to prevent blood loss or a critical reduction in tissue blood flow. In haemorrhage this can be achieved by pressure on the affected part, for example, by tourniquet, clamp, suture or thumb (every doctor has one!). When the flow reduction is due to blockage or narrowing of the relevant blood vessel, it is important to restore flow as quickly as possible by reopening the vessel (for example with balloon inflation or with stents) or by diverting blood to that region from another vessel by providing or stimulating 'collateral' vessels.

Urgency in such situations is essential, especially for organs such as the heart and brain, since these do not survive for long periods without oxygen; they cannot metabolise without it (anaerobically). If flow is not rapidly restored, brain and cardiac cells die within minutes. In the heart for example, one of the immediate effects, with a few seconds of coronary artery occlusion, is a change, a disorder in normal heart rhythm ('arrhythmias'). The most serious of these, because it is life threatening, is ventricular fibrillation. This is when the heart ceases to function as a pump and, when this takes place, blood flow to all parts of the body ceases. Later, if the heart survives this early arrhythmic period and 'normal' cardiac rhythm is restored, then those cells beyond the obstruction due to the occluded coronary vessel begin to die unless flow is gradually restored by reperfusion. This leads to 'salvage', attempting to 'save' dying cardiac cells.

When a reduction in blood flow occurs to the brain, such as occurs during a 'stroke', the resulting damage or death of brain cells leads to various disorders of brain function involving for example speech, muscle function, balance and the loss of sensations such as taste or smell. Severity depends on the site of the vessel occlusion and for how long that obstruction lasts. Because the obstruction is usually due to sticky blood cells the early use of a 'blood thinning' drug such as aspirin is recommended.

Some cellular damage occurs very soon after blood flow reduction to the heart and brain but, remarkably, seemingly full recovery can result even after a prolonged period of cerebral ischaemia. One example of this was the case of the Bolton Wanderer's footballer Fabrice Muamba who suffered a cardiac arrest during a FA Cup quarter-final against Tottenham Hotspur in 2012. He was 'technically dead' for 78 minutes. As Muamba himself said in an interview for the Times newspaper, 'what would happen if someone collapsed for ten minutes with no oxygen? The outcome would be very bad' – some understatement! – 'you would be brain damaged. But 78 minutes!' He put his amazing recovery down to a miracle. God intervened, he said, to save him, this 'miracle man', through prayer. 'Science did a part (probably cardiac resuscitation?) but God is the main part'.

How is all of this related to Christian living? The two most relevant chapters in scripture are found in John's gospel. In chapter six Jesus makes the startling, somewhat horrifying, declaration[15] that 'unless you drink his blood you have no life in you' and that his blood is 'real drink'; 'whoever drinks my blood remains in me and I in him'. As the disciples rightly remarked this is 'hard teaching' and flatly contradicted God's law. No wonder then that many of the disciples 'turned back and no longer followed him'. One can understand this reaction because, as God commanded Noah, 'you must not eat meat which has its life blood in it',[16] a

15   John 6:53-57
16   Genesis 9:4

command which later formed part of the Jewish law.[17] Blood was for the outpouring in sacrifice and was not for ingestion.

The same declaration, indeed command, to drink the blood of Jesus, comes in the gospel accounts of the Last Supper[18] and in Paul's later explanation of the meaning of Holy Communion, or Eucharist. For example, in his first letter to the church in Corinth,[19] 'this is my blood of the New Covenant poured out for the forgiveness of sins'; 'drink of it all of you'.[20] This 'drinking', of course is not to be taken literally (in Matthew 26:29 Jesus speaks of 'this fruit of the vine';[21] it is interesting that in two Old Testament passages the same word is used for both blood and wine) – 'he washed his garments in wine and clothes in the blood of grapes'.[22] This 'pouring out' of his blood was both prophesied and indeed happened on the cross.

What then did Jesus mean by drinking his blood? He is saying that unless we take his life into us, into the core of our hearts, then we have no part in him. 'Unless' he said;[23] it is obligatory. Flesh, from which blood is separated is indeed dead. Just as our physical life of the body is dependent upon the flowing of blood, no life without it, so without that life of Christ, triumphant over death, within us, there can be no spiritual life. Jesus was here talking about his death on the cross, dying for us as the Lamb of God who takes away the sin of the world, and our own sin. Indeed, dying not only as a man but as God himself; hence the startling phrase in Acts 28:28 'the blood of God' and 'the church of God which he purchased with his own blood' (the blood of God). We appropriate this sacrifice when we believe, have faith in, as a personal act, this shed blood of Christ on Calvary's Cross.

---

17 For example in Leviticus3:17; 14:15, 17:10,11 and Deuteronomy 12:23
18 Matthew 26:26-29; Mark 14:22-25; Luke 22:14-20
19 1 Corinthians 11
20 Matthew 26:27,28
21 See also Mark 14:23-25
22 Genesis 49:11; Deuteronomy 32:14
23 John 6:53

So, just as the flowing blood in our bodies provides everything each individual cell requires for life, so faith in the 'blood (of Jesus) poured out' and shed for us on Calvary, provides all we need for spiritual life.

2. Blood Cleanses

Blood not only provides all that individual cells require for life, it also removes, in the (venous) blood leaving those same cells, the waste noxious products of cellular metabolism. These waste products, if allowed to remain, would poison and kill those cells. One way of showing this is to intentionally occlude a main artery leading, for example, to a limb. When a tourniquet around the arm is tightened so as to prevent the flow of blood to the tissues below the tourniquet, and left in place for a few minutes, then pain is felt in the occluded limb especially if the fingers are exercised. The reason for this pain is a combination of the non-availability of essential nutrients and particularly, the accumulation of waste products, especially lactic acid, carbon dioxide and potassium ions. These stimulate those nerve endings responsible for the perception of pain. When the tourniquet is released, and as the blood returns to the limb (reperfusion) there is immediate pain relief as these products are washed away; the cells have thus been cleansed. These waste products are then eliminated from the body through the lungs (carbon dioxide) and the kidneys or broken down to innocuous substances in the liver.

The situation is somewhat more complex when the occluded (coronary) artery supplies the heart because, depending on the time the vessel has been occluded, life threatening arrhythmias can occur following reperfusion, sometimes leading to ventricular fibrillation and death. It is the appearance in coronary venous blood, and hence into the general circulation, of certain cardiac enzymes that serves as a diagnostic tool of cardiac damage resulting from myocardial infarction. However, careful reperfusion leads to 'myocardial salvage' and to a reduction in the number of cardiac cells that would otherwise have died.

Scripture often speaks of 'cleansing' by the blood of Jesus of all the harm caused by the 'noxious' effects of sin and which lead to spiritual death; 'the blood of Jesus cleanses from all sin'.[24] It also sanctifies (meaning 'making clean' or 'making holy') his people 'through his own blood'.[25] This thought is also apparent in the Old Testament; to cleanse a house made unclean by mildew, the blood of a dead bird, together with fresh water, when sprinkled on the home seven times, meant that the home 'will be clean'.[26] Throughout the Old Testament the sacrifices for cleansing from sin ('the blood of bulls and of goats') and reconciliation with the Holy God[27] are through the 'shedding of blood'.[28] 'Without the shedding of blood there is no forgiveness'.

Spiritually then we are 'cleansed' by the shed blood of Jesus, 'washed in the blood of the Lamb' as Sankey's old hymn has it. Indeed, this picture is a potent one in Christian hymnology. Thus, 'there is a fountain filled with blood drawn from Immanuel's veins and sinners plunged (great word!) beneath that flood lose all their guilty stains' or 'I was lost and steeped in guilt, but the blood for sinners spilt washed away my sins and set me free'. Or again, 'Not all the blood of beasts on Jewish altars slain, could give the guilty conscience peace, or wash away the stain, but Christ the heavenly Lamb takes all our sins away; a sacrifice of nobler name and richer blood than they' (Isaac Watts), words based on the letter to the Hebrews[29] We are indeed 'saved by his precious blood'. We are 'washed' in the blood,[30] made holy (white) by this blood.[31] Several times the epistle to the Hebrews speaks of the 'sprinkling' of the blood[32] or 'purging' by the blood.

24 1 John 1:7
25 Hebrews 13:12
26 Leviticus 14:49-53
27 2 Chronicles 29:24
28 Hebrews 9:13,14; 10:4, compare with Isaiah 1:11; 34:6
29 Hebrews 10:1-14
30 Revelation 1:5
31 Revelation 7:14
32 Hebrews 9:22; 11:28; 12:24; also 1 Peter 1:2

We are purchased,[33] justified,[34] redeemed,[35] brought near to God,[36] have peace with God[37] all through the blood of Jesus. The blood of Jesus 'cleanses'!

3. Blood Protects

One of the key functions of blood is defence. One such mechanism is the attempt to prevent the loss (haemorrhage) from the body of this 'sovereign principle of life', this 'priceless deposit'. When a blood vessel is injured the body is quick to respond to prevent, or reduce, further blood loss by clotting (coagulation) in order to plug the site of the damage. Almost immediately, chemical substances are released from the damaged area which attract to the site blood elements called platelets, and which also increase the flow of blood to the area. These platelets arrive in great numbers, change shape, becoming more amoeboid, then stick to and plug the damaged blood vessel wall. Later, other substances are released from these platelets that constrict the blood vessels around the site of the injury and hence reduce blood flow. Substances, such as aspirin, that inhibit these clotting mechanisms, hence increase blood loss. This also happens if platelet function is impaired.

White blood cells (leucocytes), the 'bin men of the circulation', have a number of roles to play. Some contain a large variety of substances, up to a hundred, which are involved in allergic and inflammatory responses and which lead to immunity. Invading organisms such as bacteria attract white blood cells (neutrophils) to the infected area. Here factors in blood plasma make the bacteria 'more tasty' to other cells which then engulf and digest them. These cells are therefore 'natural killer cells'. Other white blood cells (lymphocytes) are also key constituents of the immune response and have a remarkable ability to produce antibodies

---

33 Acts 20:28
34 Romans 5:9
35 Ephesians 1:7; Colossians 1:14; 1 Peter 1:18,19
36 Ephesians 2:13
37 Colossians 1:20

to many million different foreign agents that might invade the body. These have the ability to 'remember' these foreign agents such that, on further infection, there is a more rapid, and greater, defence response. Such immunity thus constitutes a major defence mechanism against infection due to bacteria, viruses and fungi.

How does this defence mechanism relate to the scriptural concept of the blood that protects? It is that Christ, through his blood, enables us to overcome those things that infect and damage us as Christian believers. In the vision of the war in heaven in the book of Revelation (chapter 12) a loud voice is heard to say 'our brothers overcame their accuser by the blood of the Lamb'. That is, because of the Cross and Resurrection, Jesus is the Victor and Conqueror who overcame forever the worst that sin and evil could do. Those who are one with Jesus share in this victory. There is nothing for which we can possibly be accused, 'who can bring any accusation'.[38] No-one can. Why? Because Jesus died and rose again and is alive for evermore; it is God who acquits and pronounces us 'not guilty'.

We work and witness for God from a position of victory. Because of his protecting blood, Jesus enables us to overcome and share in his victory; we are 'more than conquerors.'[3] So, blood and victory are linked; John[39] speaks of victory and, two verses later, speaks of 'the blood of Jesus'.

This theme of victory through the blood of Christ is evident in Christian hymnology. 'Would you over evil a victory win? There is power in the blood 'wonder working power'. This is not only the power of the blood to cleanse (such that 'the stains of sin are lost in its life-giving flow') but also to empower for service, give victory and defend us from accusation. 'Wondrous his love for me at Calvary, glorious his victory at Calvary, vanquished are death and hell. Oh, let his praises swell, ever my tongue shall tell of Calvary!' (George Perfect). They and we too, overcame by the blood of the Lamb!

38 Romans 8:34,35,37
39 1 John 5:4,6

10 KISSING

'There is a time for kissing'[1]

Kissing means to touch, press or caress with lips in order to 'greet', pay homage, reverence or love; it is an integral and precious part of Christian fellowship. It is a symbol of affection and friendship, a way to welcome or to say farewell.

Kissing takes various forms; it can be a form of greeting, especially of a woman, kissing ('pecking') on the cheeks (one or both) twice or three times – left, right, left (or in some cultures right, left, right'!) – or more formally on the hand. Or from lips to lips, although in some cultures mouth to mouth kissing is frowned upon. Indeed, mouth to mouth kissing involves not only the exchange of expired air but also of thousands of air-borne bacteria. However, as it says in Song of Solomon 'may he kiss me with the kisses of his mouth'. Sometimes this is with the anticipation of even closer bodily contact; indeed, kissing can be directed to almost any part of the body.

Kissing as a form of endearment is common when families meet. For example, the father kissed the returning prodigal son,[2] Jacob kissed Isaac,[3] Rachel[4] and Joseph's children.[5] Joseph kissed his brothers[6] and even his dead father.[7] Naomi kissed her daughters-in-law[8] and David and Jonathan kissed one another[9] to express true, loyal friendship. This was surprising as they could so easily have been enemies. Friends enriching life!

---

1 Ecclesiastes 3:5
2 Luke 15:20
3 Genesis 27:26,27
4 Genesis 29:11
5 Genesis 48:10
6 Genesis 45:15
7 Genesis 50:1
8 Ruth 1:9
9 1 Samuel 20:41

In Christian fellowship kissing is an outward sign of love, friendship and unity, of affection and goodwill. It is common when Christians meet especially for worship. It is an expression of oneness in the Lord; 'greet one another with a brotherly kiss'.[10] It is 'a kiss of love'.[11] There was to be an absence of formality, a freedom from prejudice arising from social distinctions. Moreover, it is not simply to be an expression of genuine affection but is 'holy', implying that there are three parties involved. In the early church it was almost institutionalized as a kind of mystic symbol.

One of the most famous of all scriptural kisses was when Judas betrayed Jesus, an act of treachery that led to Jesus' death - the 'kiss of death', 'the one I kiss is the man'.[12] This was both a betrayal of the Lord and indeed, of the kiss itself because of its usual association with peace and unity. Here, the Greek word means to 'kiss fervently', more demonstrative than a simple kiss of salutation; 'profuse are the kisses of an enemy'.[13] The kiss as a sign of betrayal also occurs[14] when Joab took Amasa by the beard and kissed him, an action that too led to an horrific death. In contrast, we speak of a 'kiss of life' in mouth to mouth resuscitation of someone who has stopped breathing.

---

10   1 Corinthians 16:20; 2 Corinthians 13:12
11   1 Peter 5:14
12   Mark 14:45; Luke 22:47,48
13   Proverbs 27:6
14   2 Samuel 20:9

11 REMEMBERING

'Remember Jesus Christ risen from the dead'[1]

Some time ago I was 'invited' to attend the Glasgow Memory Clinic, an organisation set up to investigate memory impairment and the possible drug treatment of the early stages of dementia. This, I hasten to add, was in response to a general invitation, to folk of a certain advanced age and not, hopefully because of any prodromal symptoms. There was the usual battery of memory tests, both oral and visual, as well as blood sampling to determine the genetic makeup with the emphasis on those genes said to predispose to severe memory impairment.

We should start with a definition. Memory is the faculty of mentally retaining impressions of past experiences and remembering is the ability to recall those stored impressions. It has been described as being 'like and old and dusty mosaic that cannot be seen until water is poured upon it'! Memory is important because it provides us with the ability not only to learn but later to modify our behaviour in the light of these experiences.

We are made up of memories; they give us a sense of who we are as individuals as we recollect past experiences, feelings and relationships. If we cannot do this we lose our sense of our own identity – a most distressing amnesia. Indeed, it is only when we begin to lose our memories that we realize that memory makes our lives; life without memories is no life at all. It has puzzled me to see some delegates at various scientific conferences I have attended wearing their name badges upside down, presumably by accident. No one can read their names, unless you stand on your head, and only they can read the name on the badge; their own. Have they really forgotten who they are?

---

1   2 Timothy 2:8

Memory involves a number of distinct brain processes; the simplest is the basic distinction between 'short-term' and 'long-term' memory. There are other distinctions; declaimed (knowing what) as compared with procedural (knowing how); episodic (what I had for breakfast) and semantic (what breakfast is for) or perhaps best of all, explicit (recollections of previous experiences) and implicit (tasks performed in the absence of conscious recollections). More of this later.

Short-term memories are transient, unstable and can vanish if interrupted. A simple example; some will remember the child's party game of determining how many objects you can remember from a tray after that tray has been removed. This is now a favourite 'game' by those involved in assessing a patient's capability to remember. This ability is reduced if that memory is interrupted by being asked to do something else – counting backwards from a hundred in sevens for example. It is clearly better to act on that memory immediately before it is impaired by the distraction of something else intervening and before that original memory vanishing into some kind of memory 'black hole'. It means that if there is a disruption during the early stages of the short-term memory process there is little chance of those tray objects being remembered in the mid to long term and that memories of recent events (sometimes called our 'working memories') can be easily erased.

What is involved in moving the memories of immediate events into our 'remote' or long-term, interacting memory stores? First, they must be important enough to be remembered; we do not need to remember those tray objects, or today's shopping list, next week or even next day. No need then to remember the events of every hour of every day of our lives, although apparently, there are some individuals who can indeed do that. Jill Price has written[2] about her ability of being able to automatically recall every day of her life from the age of fourteen on, a condition known as the hyperthymestic syndrome. Interestingly, these were memories of

2 Price, Jill, *The Woman Who Can't Forget*, New York, Free Press, 2008

what happened to her, and others, on almost any particular day; it was a superabundant autobiographical memory. However, her ability to remember learned facts, lists for example (semantic memory) was quite average. Was it good for Jill to have such a memory? Her conclusion was that such a memory was more a curse than a blessing; she was 'a prisoner of my memory'. As another Price (Fanny in Jane Austen's Mansfield Park) put it 'the memory is sometimes retentive, so serviceable, so obedient; at others so bewildered, so tyrannical'. Fortunately for most of us there is a kind of 'memory filter'. The question being 'is that memory important for us in the future?' If so then it should be retained, moved into some more permanent memory store. If not then let it disappear.

How then does the transfer of important transient short-term memory to remote, long-term memory stores take place? And, where in the structures of the brain are they laid down? Are these structures molecular (protein based) and intracellular or within neural networks, synapses? These questions, fascinating though they are, are sadly outwith the scope of the present discussion. Neither is the information derived from various surgical procedures (removal or electrical stimulation of various discrete areas of the brain) or that from clinical conditions (dementia, chronic alcoholism) appropriate in the present context, although much of what we have learnt about memory does indeed come from these sources.

Let us return to the distinction between explicit memory (retrieval from brain stores of facts or events) which has to be worked at, and implicit memory (retained memories of 'how to do things' such as how to ride a bicycle). Most of us cannot remember much, indeed anything, that happened to us up to the age of two or three years of age, which are explicit, active memories but those skills, habits learned during those very early years are retained, usually throughout life. Young children quickly learn how to stand, walk and move food from a plate to the mouth – and then swallow it. These are implicit memories and are never really forgotten. They have entered our long-term memory stores. Why? Because they are essential for normal living; they are 'protective' memories. Of course, it is not only in early childhood that such memories are laid down; I can remember the fingering for a Schubert piano sonata learnt seventy years ago (not protective – unless for any listeners – or important) but I can also remember that lovely piece by Peter Maxwell Davies learnt just last week. The memory stores are 'open all hours'!

The brain then has the ability not only to store information obtained from external stimuli (auditory, olfactory, tactile, as well as visual) but also to organise and arrange such experiences and, at a later date, to extract the information we want from those stores. The striking thing about memory is that it lasts so long, and that it is generally impervious to disruptions of brain activity such as a blow to the head; it is a permanent and indestructible form of information storage. How is it that we can recall something that happened to us both in the distant past and at a moment's notice? We would have learnt as a child a good deal of poetry. Have we done this accurately? These facts we can confirm by looking at that well-kept book of poems. Remembering events that happened to us in the past is more difficult and less accurate, unless we have some external confirming source such as a diary. One wonders for example, when people give evidence as witnesses in a court of law, whether justice is really done when months, or even years, separate the event from the recall. How well was that experience stored and then 'remembered'?

An important question for all of us concerns the possibility of improving our ability to recall selective memories. Here is some recent advice, 'tips' for remembering. Talk to yourself (which helps us to learn something new) akin perhaps to 'practice' – that piece by Maxwell Davies; go on a religious retreat; go to bed earlier (deeper sleep, more information retained – good advice before an examination since it is easier to remember facts in the morning than later in the day); certain computer games (perhaps?); clenching the fist for 90 seconds whilst reading that list and then again during recall – a form of exercise perhaps resulting in an increase in cerebral blood flow. Certainly, exercise seems to help, enhancing learning, protecting against dementia and the brain 'shrinkage' that occurs with ageing. There is experimental evidence for this; getting laboratory rats to exercise enables them to more easily learn a pathway through a maze than the more sedentary control group; it also increases the number of new cells in those areas of the brain concerned with learning and memory.

The point then about remembering is that it has a particular purpose; it is so that present actions might be informed. In other words, there are practical outworking of such memories. Interestingly, remembering in scripture is invariably a command – 'remember!' There are many things God wants us to remember. What are these things and how are we enabled to obey the command?

First God wants us to remember who He is and what He has done. Isaiah tells us[3] we are to remember that God is holy, the 'only', 'there is no other'. Jeremiah[4] tells us to remember that God 'stretched out the heavens', Solomon that he is our creator[5] and Nehemiah told the people, during the rebuilding of the walls of Jerusalem facing opposition from the local inhabitants, that they were not to be afraid but to 'remember the Lord is great and awesome'.[6] So, we are to remember who God is (the holy, 'only', great, awesome, creator) but also what He has done for His people. Thus, in David's great psalm of thanksgiving[7] he commands 'remember the wonders He has done, His marvellous works and then he reminds them of God's agreement (covenant) with His people. Many times the people of Israel are told to remember what God has done for them as part of this special relationship

---

3   Isaiah 54:5, 57:15
4   Jeremiah 32:17
5   Ecclesiastes 12:1
6   Nehemiah 4:14
7   1 Chronicles 16:8-15

he had with them. 'Remember what God did to Pharaoh and all Egypt[8] and how He brought them out of Egypt, out of the house of bondage. They are to remember too 'all the way God led them[9] and 'the days of old'.

In the New Testament the disciples were to 'remember the words of the Lord Jesus'[10] that He would rise again.[11] The written gospels testify to the fact that there were those who remembered what Jesus had said and done.

Paul too, despite the fact that he could not have heard these words, 'remembered' that the Lord Jesus said that 'it is more blessed to give than to receive'.[12] Again, after Timothy had been told to recollect his godly heritage, his family tradition and his sincere faith, he was told to remember especially 'Jesus risen from the dead'[13] that is, not just the fact of the resurrection but that the risen Lord was presently with him. We remember those who have died; memories of them are stored in our minds, but to 'remember Jesus risen from the dead' is more than that. Not just the memory of the fact about Jesus conquering death, but that he is ever present to strengthen and encourage. Timothy, in turn, was to keep on reminding the church, of which he was pastor, of these things.

The remembered facts about Jesus are summarised as a message Paul had received, remembered (!)and passed on to the Corinthian church. 'I want to speak about the gospel, which I had previously preached to you';[14] the church was urged to remember, 'I want to remind you (NIV) of the gospel' that Jesus died for our sins, was buried, raised and appeared. All these things they were to remember. So this preached gospel was to remind them of what they already knew; this is the true essence

8   Exodus 13:3
9   Deuteronomy 8:2
10   John 15:20
11   Luke 24:6,7; John 2:22
12   Acts 20:35
13   2 Timothy 2:8, 14
14   1 Corinthians 15:1 (J.B. Phillips)

of preaching – to remind people of what they already know. These facts are to be thought over, pondered in the mind. Sadly, it is said so often of the people of Israel that they 'forgot so soon what God had done for them'.

We are thus to remember the person of God, who he is, what He has done for us. And especially we are to remember Jesus. So often, problems in the Christian life, and in the church, stem from this failure to remember.

Then, we are to remember that God remembers! No need for Him to visit any memory clinic. We are in the mind and memory of God. 'I have made you, you are my servant. I will not forget you;'[15] we are engraved on His hands.[16] Of course, we remember our own hands because we look at them so often during the course of every day. The story about the man about to retire who looked forward to looking at his hands on the handle of his golf clubs six times a week and finished up looking at them in the washing up water three times a day! To be 'engraved' is almost always permanent 'marked indelibly and impressed deeply' is one definition. With the Lord we are never 'out of sight out of mind'. We are both in sight and in mind, permanently 'sealed' in God's memory.

When God remembers us He also remembers the situation in which we are placed. This is followed by action. Thus, God remembered Noah in his situation (the flood) and acted; He 'sent a wind and the waters receded'.[17] God remembered Rachel in her situation of childlessness,[18] listened to her and acted by opening her womb so that she conceived and bore a son. God remembered Abraham and sent Lot 'out of the midst of the overthrow' when He destroyed the cities of the plain.[19] So, God not only remembers us as individuals, and not only remembers the situations in which we find ourselves, but acts in these, sometimes distressing,

---

15 Isaiah 44:21
16 Isaiah 49:15, 16
17 Genesis 7:17, 24 then 8:1
18 Genesis 30:22
19 Genesis 19:29

situations. His remembering is followed by action. He acts on that memory; sent, listened, brought out, opened the womb, in those examples from Genesis.

Repetition and Recall

God understands that we need help to remember. So, how do we do it? Well, Scripture tell us how. The first way is by repetition. Less emphasis is placed in schools these days in learning 'by rote'. Multiplication tables, favourite poems; when we repeat these, the memories move from the short term to the long-term memory box. I can still remember my one and only part in a school play; just one line but it is still remembered so many years later.

How is it possible to move, by acts of repetition, information gained in the short term, like recent events, such that in time the memory of these events is consolidated and converted to long term memories? The importance of this process is that short term memories are vulnerable and subject to erasure. In my visits to the Glasgow Memory Clinic the emphasis was on the recall of words, phrases or pictures visualised a short time before.

This idea of returning often to things we need to remember must have been in the forefront of the apostle Peter's mind when he wrote his second letter.[20] He emphasises to his readers the importance of repetition; indeed Philipps, in his translation of 2 Peter 1:12 heads this section 'truth will bear repetition'. It was to recall what they already know; the words of the prophets and the command of their Lord and Saviour Jesus Christ. These folk, to whom Peter was writing, had heard God's call and 'set' (fixed) in their minds the fact that God has called and chosen them. They had chosen Jesus and Jesus had chosen them. They were 'firmly established' in the faith. Yet, despite this they still needed to be reminded. They still needed to refresh, reinforce their memories.

Then, we are to remember what we once were, 'from whence you came'. This is the thrust of Ephesians 2:11-18. We were excluded, foreigners, strangers to God's chosen community,

20   2 Peter 2:12

who had nothing to look forward to and no God to whom we could turn. We were outside the circle of God's love and purpose. We were 'far from God', at war with Him. This too we are to remember; what we once were and, just as important, what we could have become if God's grace and love had not reached down and found us. For it is only then that we can really appreciate 'the greatness of the grace which forgave and is transforming us'. Never a day should pass but that we remind ourselves of what Jesus has done for us and the wonder of salvation in Him. That is why the Jews in Berea were commended;[21] they 'searched the Scriptures daily'. This daily study of God's word is so important and for this we need a system; the study needs to be organised.

So, we are to 'stir up' our minds, to move from our transient short term memory to the long term almost permanent, deep seated part of our minds. God's word should become as natural, for example, as the ability to walk, cycle or touch type. Do we attempt to memorise Scripture? Donald Caskie, later known as the 'Tartan Pimpernel' was, at the beginning of the Second World War, the minister of the Scots Kirk in Paris. During the war he helped allied airmen, who had parachuted into enemy occupied France, to return to Britain. He was arrested by the Gestapo tortured and imprisoned in an Italian villa. In his cell he scratched with his fingernails on the plaster wall all the Scripture verses he could remember, to the blessing of the next occupier. An Hungarian pastor friend used to post on the many pillars of his church in Budapest bible verses each week for his congregation to remember. They were tested the following Sunday! A fellow lay preacher would sometimes distribute blank sheets of paper at the beginning of the Sunday evening service and ask them to write down all they could remember of the morning's sermon. Many blank faces as well as blank sheets! We are then to listen closely to God's words and store them in our hearts, or rather in our memory bank. We need to return to them, to refresh and repeat them until they become part of us.

---

21 Acts 17:11

Reminders

We also remember by things that remind us of the people we love, photos for example, or of the places we once lived in and the key events that have happened to us. In my own home there are not only photos of the family but wall hangings, pictures, wood carvings, tablecloths, china that remind us of the years we spent in Nigeria and in Hungary. One beautiful ebony carving, given to us by the Scripture Union when we left Nigeria in 1966 is of two men, one (lame) is sitting on the other (blind) man's shoulders. Apart, there are things they cannot do (one cannot walk, one cannot see) but together they can both walk and see. The point of this present was to remind us that we are still together in service for the Lord despite being 3,000 miles apart. Our task, for example, is to continue to pray for them – and they for us; we remember that whenever we look at that statue on the piano. War memorials, and that wonderful poppy display at the Tower of London in 2014, are there to remind us of those who gave their lives in the two world wars – and in wars since.

Scripture is full of reminders. In the book of Joshua (chapter 4), after the crossing of the river Jordan, the command of God to Joshua was that the people were to take twelve stones (representing the twelve tribes of Israel) from the river bed and make a cairn of them. When future generations asked the meaning of those stones they were to be reminded of the time when the 'waters of the Jordan were cut off'; the stones were to be a 'memorial', a reminder of what God had done enabling the people to 'pass over'. Similarly, in the ordinance of the Lord's Supper those very ordinary elements, bread and wine, were to lead us, when we see and partake of them, to the essential meaning behind those elements, the body and blood of the Lord[22] and what is behind, that Christ died for our sins and rose again. The elements then were physical reminders of the great spiritual truth that Christ died for our sins, rose again and is returning. Clearly, Christ had

---

22   1 Corinthians 11:23-26

realised that, as the hymn puts it, 'tell me the old, old story for we forget so soon'. So, God wants us to remember and to help us to do so has provided reminders. How much we need them!

There are other practical ways to remind us of God's truth. It is easier, for example, to remember words set to music. The psalms of the Old Testament were meant to be sung, many were written 'to the choirmaster'. Today, with paraphrases of other parts of Scripture, psalms are still sung by the congregation in Scottish churches. Some of our hymns and choruses are basically God's word set to music. Anyone who has lived in Africa will know that singing, accompanies work and travel, especially walking. They are the means of implanting in the minds of both those who sing and those who listen, essential truths about God and His activity in the world.

Lists too are a means of remembering. Those shopping lists, made with care and then left behind on the kitchen table! It took me years to realise the importance of listing those folk I need to pray for; Mondays for 'special couples', Thursdays for 'Hungarian friends', every day for the family etc. After time these lists, prayed over week by week, are no longer needed; those names are then in my long term memory. We remember also by 'association'; road signs, names of streets or names on the sides of vans, can remind us to pray for certain people. All those Campbells for example when I pass Campbell Drive or Crescent! Or mnemonics. I will never forget as a student the order by which the cranial nerves enter or leave the brain, by a simple (but unrepeatable) mnemonic. Whether coffee, chocolate, an afternoon nap or fruit juices with 'bits' help us to remember I'm not sure but we need all the help we can get to remind us what our God is like and what He has done for the world in Christ. And, is this not one reason why His Spirit has been given? 'He will bring these things (and not only 'these things') to your remembrance.[23] 'God enables us to remember'.

---

23 John 14:26

12 FORGETTING

'Forgetting what lies behind . . .'[1] but God says, 'I will not forget you'[2]

The French philosopher Henri Bergson wrote that 'the function of the brain is to enable us not to remember but to forget'. This makes good physiological, psychological and spiritual sense. A leader in the Times newspaper several years ago was entitled 'In praise of forgetfulness'; why too much memory is a dangerous thing! Forgetfulness is nature's gift, soothing away our pain and troubles. Is there not something unseemly about the obsessive desire for photographic recall and the concentration on ways to boost memory with oily fish, lemon balm, rosemary and mint as well as with the increasing variety of drugs and 'techniques' (starting with that knot in the handkerchief) developed to assist in correcting memory dysfunction, turning hazy, fuzzy memories into sharp, detailed focus? Although, if Bergson is correct, then some of us have good functioning brains; we can certainly forget. No problem!

The brain then has but a finite capacity for memories so it is important for us to forget inappropriate, meaningless information. Given the overwhelming flood of information that pours into our brains minute by minute it is important to forget some things just as it is important to remember some. For example, does it really matter if names simply disappear or that faces fade into many shades of grey? This kind of forgetfulness, that shopping list left by accident on the kitchen table, the continual hunt for keys or spectacles or what comes next in that story we started telling, may be a trifle embarrassing but is probably relatively unimportant. To some variable extent this occurs in all old people; I write as a man

---

1 Philippians 3:13
2 Isaiah 49:15

in his eighties! However, although it might be irritating to have forgotten where you have left your car keys it is important not to have forgotten what they are for!

Are there ways to enable us to forget? Do we have to remember to forget? The philosopher Immanuel Kant was systematically robbed by his servant Lampe and eventually dismissed him. But Lampe was sorely missed. Kant wrote in his journal – 'remember to forget Lampe'. He was training his 'forgettery'. It became the reverse process to remembering where, in order to remember, we revive that image, hold it fast, dwell on it, repeat and repeat again. To forget then is to reverse this process; when that hurt comes back into our memory we need to turn our minds way from it, dwell instead on something else, like God's goodness or even trivial things; for me attempting to recall the Köchel numbers of all Mozart's twenty-seven piano concertos! Or pray about it; short prayers though since in long prayers you tend to dwell on that thing you need to forget. The aim is for those things we want to forget to vanish into memory's black hole and not to perpetually relive that painful past.

There is one form of forgetting however that is much more serious than those examples given above. This is when forgetfulness is an illness and where the inability to remember becomes incapacitating. This is called amnesia. It can follow acute brain injury but is more commonly due to degenerative changes in those parts of the brain, for example specialised regions of the cerebral cortex such as the hippocampus and the amygdala, that are thought to be concerned with the 'laying down of memories'. This tragic form of forgetting has vast health and social implications that are outside the scope of this chapter.

It is surely true that anyone with an obsession with the past 'forgets' to savour the present. Now, most of our forgetting is accidental; indeed, one definition is to 'omit accidentally'! However, forgetting in scripture is a different matter altogether. This is an active and purposeful putting aside of events in the past that we really ought to remember.

One of the difficulties the psalmist had on occasions was the feeling that God had forgotten him. The heartfelt cry of David[3] 'how long will you forget me, O Lord? For ever?' And that recurrent question 'why'?[4] Is it possible for God to forget? The answer surely comes from Isaiah; when speaking about God's people he says that although yes, it is sadly possible for a mother to forget her child, God says 'I will not forget you', 'you will not be forgotten by me'.[5] We are engraved on his hands.

But does God then have a 'forgettery'? He does. He forgets our sins. 'I am the one who wipes out your transgressions and I will remember your sins no more.'[6] If our sins are confessed and forsaken, if repentance and sorrow are deep, lasting and meaningful, if we have made restitution and put things right, and if we have accepted that Jesus died on the cross, bearing those very sins, then God has forgiven and forgotten.[7] They have been 'buried in the deepest sea', separated from us 'as far as the east is from the west'[8] – some distance! – and put behind his back[9] where we cannot see them and neither can God! They are 'blotted out', covered, hidden, swept away, wiped out, forgotten.

It is important to note that this forgetfulness is not, unlike ours, accidental and unintentional but active and definite. This means that we too should forget those sins and put them behind us. This is part of what the apostle Paul meant when he wrote of 'forgetting (leaving) things behind'. After all, Paul had a stained past with much to be forgiven but if God had forgotten his many sins he too should forget them. Of course, Paul regretted the pride and bigotry of this earlier life, and his persecution of the church, but he did not brood over a past that could not be altered. So

---

3 Psalm 13:1
4 Psalm 42:9
5 Isaiah 44:21; 49:15
6 Isaiah 43:25
7 Hebrews 8:12; 10:17
8 Psalm 103:12
9 Isaiah 38:17

too with us. Those sins are to be left well behind; we should not attempt to drag them back from the past. To do so would cast doubt on the reality of God's forgiveness.

There are other things too that we should actively forget. Those hurtful things done against us. If our sins are forgiven and forgotten, then we too need to forgive and forget those things done against us. Churches are full of spiritual cripples, paralysed by the grudges, bitterness, jealousies of the past because of the inability to both forgive and forget. To say, 'I can forgive but can never forget' is not true forgiveness. If we have been hurt by what someone has said or done in the past, then we must not allow that to poison our relationships. There is a story about the Nazi leader Ribbentrop, someone prone to 'putting his foot in it', that he could never forget the embarrassment of the 'fun' made of him when he was, in the 1930's, the German ambassador to Britain (he was nicknamed 'Herr Brickendrop'). This festered a deep hatred of all things British. He could not put that part of his past behind him. Wounds left without treatment can become septic. And sepsis still has a 60–70% mortality.

But how is it possible to forget? To put the past behind? I am always intrigued by the Old Testament story of Joseph which surely teaches how this is possible with God's help. Joseph was nearly murdered by his brothers, was sold into slavery, falsely accused, imprisoned and then forgotten by the man whose dream he had interpreted, 'yet the cupbearer did not remember Joseph'.[10] He was forgotten. Intentional or accidental? Yet, later when his first son was born he named him Manasseh[11] because 'God has made me forget all my troubles and (note!) my father's house' presumably including all those hurtful, jealous brothers and what they had done to him. So, Joseph's experience was that with God's help he was able to put behind him those terrible, hurtful experiences that originated from his brother's jealousy. For the Christian too there should be something else enabling us to 'forgive and forget';

10   Genesis 40:51
11   Genesis 41:51

it is the love and example of Jesus. But, I wonder, is this truly possible? Can forgiveness always be separated from forgetting? Isn't it always possible, if we so wish or are prompted, to 'drag back' issues from the past? And isn't this simply because, unlike God, our abilities both to forget and to remember are imperfect?

However, in this respect there is a moving example recorded in a book by Bishop Festo Kivengere called *Revolutionary Love*.[12] In it he describes how, following the murder by Idi Amin of his friend and 'beloved brother' Janini Luwum, the Archbishop of Uganda, he and his wife had to flee Uganda. Travelling over the mountains they eventually arrived in London. The first Good Friday found Festo in All Souls Church in London, next to the BBC, at a meditation on the seven last words of Jesus from the cross. As the first of these words was read, 'Father forgive them for they do not know what they are doing'[13] Festo heard the Lord saying to him 'you cannot forgive Amin? You know he could have been one of those soldiers driving those nails into my hands'.

'Yes, Lord he could have been,' Festo replied.

'Do you think I would have prayed, "Father forgive them – all except Idi Amin?"'

'No master, even he would have come within the embrace of your boundless love'.

That love enabled Festo to forgive and put behind, in mind as well as heart, his terrifying hurtful experience and later he wrote a somewhat controversial book entitled 'Why I love Idi Amin'. He put it simply – 'God made me forget'. And it is surely only that sacrificial love and example of Jesus that enables us to 'forgive and forget'.

---

12 Kivengere, Festo, *Revolutionary Love*, Fort Washington, USA, Christian Literature Crusade, 1985
13 Luke 23:34

13 AGEING

'The years of our life, so teach us to number our days'[1]

The ageing process is slow (commencing at birth!) universal, inevitable and irreversible, a cumulative decline ending in death. Worldwide, by the year 2050 there will be two billion people over the age of 65, a fact that has profound implications for the delivery of health and social care. As Jesus said to Peter 'when you are old . . .'[2] But what is old, what is ageing? It is the physical body wearing out, those physiological and anatomical changes that are the natural consequence of the passage of time. The results are clear to see and experience! The years of this life speed forward like the pages of a good book being flicked at an ever increasing rate to its ultimate denouement!

There is a very pertinent description of ageing in the book of Ecclesiastes (chapter twelve), a passage which it seems Shakespeare had in mind when he put, into the mouth of the melancholy Jacques in 'As you like it',[3] words about the effects of ageing. The mental effects, 'a second childishness', and the physical ('sans teeth, sans eyes, sans taste, sans everything'), the shrunken body, the change in the voice, the inevitable decline. In the book of Ecclesiastes we have a graphic description of declining faculties and failing strength, the inevitable toll on the body, like a 'trembling' house (12:3); the bent frame and slow walk (like a 'grasshopper drags itself along' 12:5). The faculties too; 'grinders (teeth) cease' because they are few. The eyesight declines ('those who look through windows' (perhaps a description of loneliness) 'are dim' (12:3). Mental collapse; 'the doors on the street shut', a picture of isolation, 'the keys of the house tremble', perhaps a

---

1 Psalm 90:10,12
2 John 21:18
3 Act 2 Scene,7

picture of anxiety. There is fear ('terrors' 12:5), sadness ('wailers' 12:5), lack of pleasure (12:1), the body 'broken and shattered' (12:6). Maybe too, the broken pitcher and broken wheel (12:6) speak graphically, and respectively, of urinary incontinence and of cardiac failure. The 'broken wheel' (12:6) is also evidence of a deterioration in brain function, so sadly now a common occurrence in the elderly. Nothing new 'under the sun'! The ending death, the ultimate certainty. All this an intrinsic picture of life. It is a picture too of God neglected and hence the capacity for true joy lost. Hopeless? Well, death is making way for an untried generation and our legacy is in the genes (something of us) passed down the generations, a picture for the Jewish writer Jonathan Sacks, of 'eternal life'.

I remember way back in the 1960s hearing a radio interview with the great Austrian orchestral conductor Bruno Walter. Mozart apparently 'never went to bed without thinking that he might not be alive in the morning'. Mozart used the word *gluckheiligkeit* (beatitude) when talking about death, which 'he did daily', to 'express his nearness to death (he died at the age of 35) and at the same time nearness to God'. As Walter then said 'it is the same, death is the door to eternity and what is behind eternity. Death is the door'. For the Christian believer death is a 'going home' to another 'house', to a room prepared.[4] As Michael Eaton (in his Tyndale Commentary)[5] puts it, 'could it be that the hideous purposeless and seeming futility of life stems from the fact that one will not believe in a God who is the 'rewarder of those who diligently seek him' and who do not respond to God's incredible generosity in sending his Son Jesus to give eternal life'. Spiritual life only begins in the physical life when we are 'born again' of God's Spirit. This life continues through death into eternity.

What then happens during the ageing process? Well, first it is time dependent. The World Health Organisation (WHO) criteria is

---

4 John 14:2
5 Eaton, M.A., *Ecclesiastes*, Leicester UK, Inter-Varsity Press, 1983

that an elderly adult, a 'senior', is any person over the age of sixty. It is then classified; there are those in the third (60 to 74 years old) and fourth (75 to 89 years of age) stages, then come the 'longer livers' (90 to 99 years old) and the 'centenarians' (over 100 years old). Age is thus not necessarily associated with termination, although of course it eventually ends in physical death. So, this chronological age (age in years) is not the same as biological age, which is a physiological concept depending on the functional condition of various bodily processes, an age dependent process of bodily deterioration. This is greatly accentuated by disease, especially when this effects a series of organs simultaneously. The process can also be accelerated by factors such as high blood pressure, obesity, lack of physical activity or addiction to alcohol and other drugs, as well as by psychological factors such as loneliness, anxiety, depression and stress.

Throughout history there have been attempts to slow or reverse this process, the searching for the 'elixir of eternal life'. The play by Bernard Shaw, 'Back to Methuselah' and Gounod's opera 'Faust' are examples of this fascination with prolonging life. Janacek's opera 'The Makropulos Case', a comedy written to 'convey a sense of optimism and consolation', is the story of Emelia Marty, a woman who knew the secret of the 'elixir of life' and who cheats death and lives for three hundred years! Janacek wrote of her 'the terror of inner feelings of a human being who will never cease to breathe; complete despair which wants nothing and expects nothing. Perhaps it is optimistic to say that it is a good thing to live for seventy years and a bad thing to live for three hundred!' In fact, Janacek wrote almost all of his major works after the age of seventy! We cannot will to be something mightier than God has made us; we must accept the role allotted to us in the scheme of creation.

The changes resulting from ageing can be separated into those affecting the physical body and those due to psychological factors which influence the mind. Physically, we lose height as we grow older; I was surprised to learn during a recent visit to the hospital, that I was now, at the age of 83, only 5 foot and 3 inches tall compared to my earlier height of 5 foot 7 inches! This is due to the decrease in the height of the vertebrae. As we grow older we walk more slowly, with shorter steps and a tendency to 'drag' the feet. Running becomes difficult. The skin, like the paper and ink on the pages of an old book, wrinkles. Hair turns grey, due to lack of melanin, and tends to fall out. The nails get harder making them more difficult to cut.

This ageing process involves all the cells of the body and includes a shrinkage in cell size (called atrophy), leading to a deterioration in function especially in organs such as the heart, kidneys and lungs. In the heart, there are changes in structure which include an increase in the size and thickness of the wall of the left ventricle, a sign of developing heart failure. There are changes too in cardiac electrical activity, for example a more rapid rate of beating of the thin walled atria, a condition called atrial fibrillation. Disorders due to atherosclerosis result in a narrowing of the blood vessels, leading to increases in blood pressure. There is also a restriction in the blood flow to the heart through the coronary arteries, with a resulting inability to match cardiac oxygen demand to supply under conditions of exercise and stress.

There are changes too in the eyes, making it more difficult to focus. This is due to dryness, a yellowing of the lens and a decrease in the size of the pupils, making reactions to changes to dark and light slower. There may also be changes in taste, initially to the sensations of salt and sweet. Because the mouth produces less saliva, dryness and difficulties in swallowing occur. Sometimes there are marked changes in the ability to smell. This is the result of a diminishing number of nasal nerve endings. A more pronounced change also occurs in hearing, especially to the higher frequencies. The practical implications of this are that conversation becomes more difficult, especially where there is background noise, and speech becomes poorly articulated (mumbling). Surtitles on the TV are now essential. However, on the plus side, these are often the funniest things on television!

These changes in hearing are reasonably easily corrected following the rapid advances in hearing aid technology.

There are two particular dangers of ageing. The first is frailty, defined as vulnerability to sudden changes in health triggered by a stress event; it is a consequence of age-related physiological decline. About half of people over the age of eighty-five fall into this category of 'being frail', with an increased risk of falls due to a decrease in bone mass and strength. The condition of osteoporosis is when the bones become more fragile and porous due to the loss of mineral content, especially calcium. This leads to a greater risk of fracture since, when pressure is applied to a bone greater than it can bear, the bone splits or breaks (fractures). Balance and gait impairment are also major features of frailty and both are risk factors for falling. One result of falling is a failure to adapt to the environment often leading to a loss of independence. This tendency to fall with age up to eighty is more common in men than in women. Thereafter, interestingly, after this age the tendency to fall decreases.

The second danger of ageing is psychological. The danger is for the mind to sink gradually, as the years go by, into a smaller, narrower life. A tendency to become more anxious about everyday things and of being frustrated about 'things we can no longer do'. The orchestral conductor Osmo Vanska once wrote about the composer Jan Sibelius's autobiographical sixth symphony. This was written when Sibelius was an 'ageing man', when he felt his incapacities; 'the ideas are still there but cannot now be reached'. Yet how old was he when he wrote this symphony in 1922? Not yet sixty!

It is clear that depression and dementia are not necessary consequences of 'mental ageing'. The risk of such is heightened by isolation, loneliness and by limiting activity to 'in and around the home', sometimes described as 'shelterville'. This risk is reduced by social activity, reading, puzzles, learning something new and by creative and spiritual activities which increase cognitive reserve, those mental skills we develop as a result of past intellectual, emotional and cultural activities. A sense of adventure! 'Roaming in the gloaming' in the later years! The danger of decline is basically a failure of the human 'inner man', the heart or centre of human life, to grow even larger and more generous. This is because it has failed to perceive that development of mind and spirit. Yet this is still possible! It depends on giving rather than receiving, on losing rather than gaining. There are wonderful scriptural examples of this as we shall see.

However, we do need to remember that even being at an advanced age can be fulfilling, sometimes exciting. It is not all 'doom and gloom'. There is still much that can be done. I revise this chapter (yet again!) on the day the Duke of Edinburgh announced he was 'standing down' as he approached his 96th birthday, his tongue in cheek explanation being that he now finds 'standing up' somewhat 'more problematic'! Yet, even at that age his activities were not coming to an end; he could just be more selective about those occasions he would attend. In other words, still contributing!

The brain shrinks with age with consequences such as reduced spontaneity of thought, a decreased ability for problem solving, memory loss (especially of more recent events) and decision making. There may also be a change in language; a reduced vocabulary or an inability to choose 'the right word'. It is memory loss that is the most troublesome. But although you do not need to worry where you put the car keys, you do need to worry if you cannot remember what they are for!

I recently came across a wonderful song by Graham Kendrick which begins with the words 'For the joys and for the sorrows'. I have no idea what the author was going through when he wrote this song in 1994 but it reflects so accurately some of the spiritual problems associated with ageing – the 'troubled mind', the disappointments, the weakness of the body, the sleeplessness, 'the burdens of the day' and the 'not yet answered prayer'. It is like a 21st century psalm. However, there is also acceptance of his present situation – 'the truth of what I am'. The chorus goes 'In this I have Jesus' and the 'strength to fight and win'. It seems to me reading and singing this song, that Graham Kendrick has proved that for him Jesus has been sufficient for all these varied experiences of life – 'for THIS I have Jesus'.

Ageing in Scripture

There are several scriptural examples of men (never women!) making hasty or incorrect decisions when they 'became old'. Thus, Samuel when he 'became old'[6] made his two sons, Joel and Abijah, judges over Israel despite their reputation as 'men who did not walk in God's ways but turned aside after gain, taking bribes and perverting justice'. This bad decision became obvious to others and was put down to Samuel's age.

Again, there are several indications that King David, in marked contrast to his earlier years, found decisions, or certainly the right ones, more difficult to make as he grew older. First, after the rebellion of his son Absalom (the story is in 2 Samuel chapters 13 through to 16) there was indecision regarding the relationship between Mephibosheth and Ziba.[7] Hasty and bewildered, David gave Saul's estate to the cunning Ziba before first ascertaining all the facts; a decision he partially reversed later when the facts became known. A case perhaps of compromise resulting from a half-hearted decision made in haste.

Later still, his decision to 'number the people'[8] despite the query from Joab ('why does my Lord the king delight in this thing'), was a decision that David later recognised as a sin. Then, when 'old and advanced in years' and 'at ease with himself', he hesitated in deciding who was to be his successor.[9] Amidst the machinations and divisions in his kingdom (even the priests were divided), David delayed before pronouncing Solomon as the new king. But why the delay? An earlier decision might have headed off the divisions in his kingdom.[10]

---

6   1 Samuel 8:1,5
7   2 Samuel 16:1-4; 19:24-30
8   2 Samuel 24:1-3, 10, 11
9   1 Kings 1:1
10   1 Kings 1:7,8,29,30

Another example of the spiritual effects of ageing comes in the tragic story of the 'old prophet' in 1 Kings 13. This man certainly had all the hallmarks of complacency and decay within him. Out of jealousy for a courageous younger man who 'came with the word of God', the 'old prophet' caused the younger man to stumble and to disobey the Lord's clear word to him.[11] Was this jealousy of a younger man's success and courage because he had received 'the word of God' and that the 'older' prophet' had not? An example perhaps of slackness in God's service in later life? The younger man had done what he, the older prophet, should have done. A clear and dramatic warning for those who are older not to denigrate the young but to encourage them in faith and service. This story is in marked contrast to the incident in the previous chapter when king Rehoboam turned for advice to his young men and failed to act on the sound advice of 'the old men' who had advised his father.[12]

Later in the history of God's people even 'good kings' like Hezekiah and Josiah found decisions difficult late in their lives. Hezekiah made the foolish decision to welcome, and then to show, the envoys from Babylon 'all his treasure house'.[13] As Hezekiah said to Isaiah, 'there was nothing in my storehouses that I did not show them'. Foolish? The prophet told him what God thought of this foolish decision.[14] The result would be that 'your treasure, and your sons too, will be carried away to Babylon'. Josiah too, after a wonderful reign, so different from that of most of his predecessors, in 'the end' made the foolish decision to join with the Pharaoh of Egypt. The consequence was that he was killed in battle.[15] But why 'go up' to meet Pharaoh in the first place? A disastrous decision at the end of his life. These foolish old men!

But even more serious are those who, in old age, turn away from the Lord. Solomon, despite his prayer life,[16] his granted request for

11   1 Kings13:9
12   1 Kings 12: 6-14
13   2 Kings 20:12-19
14   2 Kings 20:16-18
15   2 Kings 23:29
16   1 Kings 8:13-54

wisdom,[17] his long reign[18] and his work in rebuilding the Temple, 'did not fully follow the Lord and did evil in God's sight'.[19] Solomon began well, but the affairs of this world, his sexual appetite,[20] his disobedience and his worship of false idols later in life, 'when he was old'[21] led Solomon to be described as one who 'was not wholly true to the Lord his God'.[22] How tragic it is to begin well and end so badly. How old, I wonder, was Demas, who after much service to the church, also 'turned away' and deserted Paul, because he was 'in love with this present world'.[23] Was this due to old age? The prayer attributed to Sir Francis Drake, the sixteenth century English admiral, comes to mind. 'There must be the beginning of any great matter but it is the continuing to the end, until it is thoroughly finished, that yields the true glory'. 'Let him (or her) who thinks he stands take heed lest he fall'[24] we might say, especially in old age!

In contrast, how good it is to turn to scriptural examples of those who did 'continue to the end' and indeed, seemed to blossom in old age! Think of Joseph who, after all the ups and downs of his life, finished well, kindly and forgiving to the end.[25] Then there was Caleb who, in earlier days had encouraged Moses and the people[26] and when well into his eighties[27] 'wholly followed the Lord'. Joshua too, after a lifetime of service, when 'old and well advanced in years'[28] encouraged his people and charged them to 'choose this day whom you will serve'. Then he continued with his own testimony, 'as for me and my house we will serve the Lord'.[29]

17 1 Kings 4:29-34
18 1 Kings 11:42
19 1 Kings 11:6,9
20 1 Kings 11:2,3
21 1 Kings11:4
22 1 Kings 11:5
23 2 Timothy 4:10
24 1 Corinthians 10:12
25 Genesis 50:21
26 Numbers 13:30; 14: 6,24
27 Joshua 14:6-14
28 Joshua 23:2
29 Joshua 24:14,15

He died at one hundred and ten years still continuing! Barzillai, 'very aged', over eighty years old,[30] and despite the loss of his physical senses (hearing, taste)[31] supported David, at a critical time in the king's life and was later blessed and kissed by the king.

In the New Testament we have the wonderful example of Anna,[32] perhaps the supreme example of how to deal spiritually with the problem of ageing. She was really old! Over one hundred years perhaps; certainly at least eighty-four. She was probably engaged at twelve and married at nineteen, a widow, perhaps childless, but in her old age certainly not finished! A woman whose life was characterised by worship, thanksgiving, prayer, fellowship with likeminded folk like Simeon, and still open to hearing God's voice. Still thinking about the future (at eighty-four!) still 'looking forward', vibrantly active in her faith, with the God given insight to recognise who Jesus was! This doesn't fit in with the current thinking about old age of being 'retired, comfortable and having a well-earned rest'! Anna challenges all our presumptions about the elderly. Not useless, not undervalued but still maturing and used by God. Still 'available'! No 'well-earned rest' for Anna!

There is still in our churches, and elsewhere in the wider world, the danger of undervaluing the elderly. They have much to contribute to the life of a vibrant, worshipping church fellowship. How can we promote their ministry and use the experience of life of 'senior members' who continue to be radical disciples of Jesus? We need actively to involve those who are 'ever full of sap and green' and who continue to declare that the Lord is upright and their 'rock'. And for those of us now in declining years the wonderful and insightful Psalm 71 should especially be in our minds and on our lips!

---

30 2 Samuel 19:32,35
31 2 Samuel 19:35
32 Luke 2:36-38

14 SEEING

Before we look at each of the five senses separately, perhaps it is relevant to explain simply the intricacies of the human peripheral nervous system. This is divided into two main parts, the sensory (afferent) system that conveys, by electrical signals, information to the brain from receptors responding to sound, sight, touch, smell etc. and which terminate as myriads of minute nerve fibres in the receiving (sensory) part of the brain, the sensory cortex. The resultant response is to conduct (efferent) nerve impulses away from the brain to the various 'effector' organs such as muscles and glands.

'He who formed the eye'[1] 'gives man sight'[2]

The genius of normal human vision is that it is the main route to the mind ('the mind's eye') and 'wisdom to the soul'. Indeed, the central position of the eyes in the face has led to the idea that the 'self' (the 'I') is equated with the eye which is, of all facial features, inherently the most expressive. Seeing underpins our understanding of the world around us and, despite the enormous complexities involved, we know more about vision than about almost any other high-level function of the brain. Nevertheless, much about 'seeing' remains deeply mysterious. This pre-eminence of vision among the five senses is supported by the fact that it is the organ of supreme elaboration and sensitivity. However, the real business of vision is the brain; the visual cortex at the back of the brain.

The eye is basically an organ for collecting light. Shaped like a ball, it has three coats or layers – the outer tough sclerotic coat is modified at the front to form the transparent cornea; the middle (choroid) coat, has a nutritive function and is highly vascular; the

1 Psalm 94:9
2 Exodus 4:11

innermost coat, the retina, is the really functioning part of the eye because of its sensitivity to light waves. The eyeball itself is fluid filled – the aqueous and vitreous humour – between which is the elastic lens, which focuses the light waves on the most sensitive part of the retina. The lens is suspended by small cords or ligaments and by the ciliary muscles, which enable its shape to be changed depending upon whether the object is near or far away. This allows us to focus. All the media in the eye through which the light has to pass are transparent; if this transparency is lost (for example if there is opacity of the lens – cataract) then vision is impaired.

The amount of light entering the eye is regulated by the coloured iris. The image of the object 'seen' reaches the retina macula, a minute patch about a third of a mm wide, a filmy substance like an 'inside out' brain, it is a tangle of light-sensitive cells (stimulated by electromagnetic waves) called cones, around which are the even more sensitive, but less discriminating, rods. The object observed actually arrives at the retina like a patchwork of tints; it is the brain that works out what these tints mean; what particular object is 'seen'.

Vision thus involves the detection of light. The light, electromagnetic, non-ionizing radiation with wavelengths between 400 and 750 nanometres, is reflected from the surfaces of objects which absorb different parts of the spectrum. Changing the wavelength composition enables us to detect colour. This depends on the interaction between the different kinds of cone cells in the retina which respond to different parts of the visual spectrum, red, green and blue. With this trichromatic system it is possible to distinguish between over a million degradations of colour. Indeed, some women possess an additional photopigment with a resultant increase in colour perception and differentiation. My wife's ability to 'match' clothes with different shades of 'redness' is superior to my own; her red is not my red!

Stimulation of the rods and cones leads to the release of a chemical transmitter which results in a change in electrical potential.

These electrical signals then pass to the sensory visual cortex of the brain by means of bundles of the million or so nerve fibres which comprise the optic nerve. These signals are then processed in the centre for integration in the sensory cortex, which then, together with information from other sensory organs, such as the ears and the neck muscles, enables us to direct our gaze. The perception of form (shape), movement and colour occur independently of each other in different areas of the brain. These are then wonderfully brought together and analysed so that from a blurred patchwork of coloured tints we can recognise a particular object. What our eyes 'see', for example, is a blotch of green; but the recognition of it as a particular object, a tree for example, is the function of the cerebral cortex. This is where the shape and colour of this 'blotch' is analysed.

The real business of vision is thus undertaken by the brain. A baby may see a tree as 'green' but it does not recognise what it is; a mother's face appears as an off-white blur. It is only later, when the brain now sees that blur as belonging to part of mother, that recognition occurs and the image stored as a visual memory. That blur was not a problem of the eye but of the brain relating what was 'seen' to experience. For example, my great-granddaughter when very young was fascinated by the face of a clock, but how does she distinguish between the face of an inanimate object and the face of her parents? And how, and at what stage in her development, does she distinguish between the faces of her mother, father, grandparents and her many and varied aunties?

This ability to distinguish between faces is then a function of the brain and depends on the growth of nerve networks between the various parts of the cerebral cortex. Did something similar happen when the blind man of Bethsaida healed by Jesus[3] saw first 'men as trees walking'? The healing was in this case a gradual process, and was of the mind as well as of the eyes. Perhaps the healing by Jesus of the man born blind man in John's gospel

---

3 Mark 8:22-25

(chapter nine) is another example of a more gradual healing; the man first had a combination of saliva and mud put on his eyes but then had to wash in the Pool of Siloam. It was not the washing but Jesus who healed the man, requiring obedience on his part. Did it require more time for those nerve connections in the visual cortex to occur even in these miracles of Jesus?

What is remarkable, indeed mysterious, is why electrical signals arriving at the visual cortex are experienced as 'sight' (vision) whereas similar electrical signals travelling down similarly constructed nerve fibres, arriving at another part of the brain (for example the auditory cortex) are registered as 'hearing'.

It can happen that information from one sense organ can 'overlap' with another. For example, touch, hearing and sight. An example of this is a condition called synaesthesia in which the perception of colour and sound (music) are combined. Some composers, such as Scriabin, Messiaen and Michael Torke were said to have 'key colour synaesthesia', each musical key being associated with a particular colour; yellow for B flat major and D major with red. However, for some individuals, D major is associated with green or, for others, blue!

Scripture is full of references to eyes and sight (or lack of it). Eyes can be beautiful[4], weak[5], bright[6], like doves[7], 'pools' or like a flame of fire[8]. Sometimes, and significantly, the eye is a key component of visions; the cherubim were for Ezekiel 'full of eyes'[9] as were the four living creatures, and the wheels beside them.[10] The four living creatures in John's vision were 'full of eyes in front and behind'.[11] These were visions of the

4   1 Samuel 16:12
5   Leah in Genesis 29:17
6   Jonathan in 1 Samuel 14:27, 29
7   Song of Solomon 4:1, 5:12
8   Revelation 1:14, 2:18
9   Ezekiel 10:12
10 Ezekiel 1:18
11 Revelation 4:8

indescribable living God. Totally beyond comprehension. One wonders what nerve connections were involved!

There is however another aspect of 'seeing God'. Paul reminds us that we look not at the 'seen' but at the 'unseen'; this with the eye of faith.[12] These 'unseen things' are, unlike this present and 'seen' world, eternal and are 'really permanent'. Faith itself is a conviction, an assurance, of 'things not seen'.[13] A good Old Testament example comes in the story of Elisha.[14] Surrounded by danger Elisha's servant saw only the army of the enemy surrounding his master. He could see only the immediate present situation and, of course, he was greatly afraid ('Alas, my master, what shall we do?'). Only after Elisha had prayed that great prayer, 'O Lord, open his eyes' did he realise the presence with them of the living, powerful God; 'fire' is, throughout scripture, a symbol of the Lord's presence.[15] Of course, the enemy was still present and the servant could still see them but now he could see something else, 'beyond' that present situation. And, it is a prime function of the church to remind people of the 'unseen'. There are other examples. Stephen, at his martyrdom saw 'heaven opened, the glory of God and Jesus standing',[16] he saw beyond (that wonderful Scottish word 'ayont') his present predicament, those stones being hurled at him, to the 'unseen'.

So, then what does it mean to 'see God'? First there are those who have seen, listened, met and handled Jesus in the flesh.[17] Then, there were those who had visions of God like Daniel, Ezekiel and Zechariah. Again, there are those who, even today, have had 'out of death' experiences which have included 'visions' of heaven. Lastly, there are the many whose spiritual eyes, initially closed, have been opened by the Holy Spirit and that prayer 'open my eyes that I might see' has been answered.

12 2 Corinthians 4:18
13 Hebrews 11:1
14 2 Kings 6:8-17
15 as in Exodus 3:2; 13:21
16 Acts 7:56
17 1 John 1:1

Thus, in the wonderful prayer of Paul comes the request that the Christians in Ephesus might have the 'eyes of the heart' (or 'understanding' in the AV) enlightened, a deep illumination, and that they might experience the hope of their calling, the riches of their inheritance and the greatness of God's power.

All this experience coming from the opening of their spiritual eyes.[18] In this context 'heart' includes affections without excluding intelligence; it is indeed the centre of the whole personality, the 'core' of being, the 'inner man', the 'inward self'. In other words our inner eyes are to be opened so that we can grasp God's truth. This opening of our spiritual eyes comes to us primarily as we meet God in the words of scripture and in answer to the prayer 'open our eyes Lord we want to see Jesus'. We see him in the word.

God Sees!

God is all knowing, all wise and all seeing. This concept of an active, watching God comes throughout scripture. There is nothing he does not notice in the world he has made. He sees 'all men',[19] the 'eyes of the Lord run to and throw throughout the whole earth',[20] he 'looks down' on the children of men, on all nations.[21] God has a watching brief, he sees the direction we take, our steps and our ways.[22] There is no hiding from God, he sees in the secret place.[23] Nothing escapes the eyes of God. God sees me![24] The emphasis in these verses is on 'all' our ways, he is looking after those who fear and acknowledge him[25] with the idea of protection. He looks down in love. God sees our particular situation. He understands and sympathises. Thus, he

---

18 Ephesians 1:18
19 Jeremiah 32:19
20 2 Chronicles 16:9
21 Psalm 14:2, 53:2, 66:7, 113:6
22 Job 34:21; Proverbs 5:21; Jeremiah 32:19
23 2 Kings 6:12
24 Genesis 16:13
25 Job 36:7; Psalm 33:18; 34:15

is open to our requests to him.[26] Indeed, often we ask God who sees 'in secret'[27] to see where we are, to 'open his eyes and see',[28] especially in situations of great sadness when he will, in love, answer.

Blindness

The dictionary definition of 'blind' is 'without sight' (legally blind). In fact, it rarely means the complete absence of the ability to perceive light. Indeed, one definition of blindness is 'that a person can be certified (as blind) if they cannot see sufficiently to do any work for which eyesight is essential'. So, whether someone can be classified as blind depends on their visual acuity, in practice whether they are able to distinguish letters of the alphabet at a certain distance. Of course, someone totally blind cannot see the screen at all.

Blindness has a variety of causes. Old age is one such, as the bible recognises; Isaac,[29] Israel[30] and Eli[31] all had defective vision. They had 'eyes dim with age'. Their eyesight 'had begun to grow dim' such that 'they could not see'. Probably they could all see something but failed to distinguish correctly one person from another; Isaac failing to distinguish between his two sons. One cause of blindness in these 'ancients' could have been age-related macular degeneration or the presence of cataracts. Other causes of blindness include infective diseases (infection with chlamydia affects about 500 million people worldwide), glaucoma, diabetes and damage to the visual cortex resulting, for example, from a stroke.

However, as we discover from scripture, there is another definition of 'blindness'; ignorance arising from a failure to

---

26 1 Peter 3:12
27 Matthew 6:4
28 Lamentations 3:49, 50; Daniel 9:8
29 Genesis 27:1
30 Genesis 48:10
31 1 Samuel 3:2; 4:15

appreciate or accept God's word. So this analogy of physical blindness is carried over into the spiritual realm. It is the failure to see, completely or in part, spiritual truth. Such individuals had physical eyes but could not 'see' or understand what God wants to say to them. In most cases this is self-inflicted, they have 'closed their eyes that they might not see'[32] through prejudice (closed minds) and sin. Although sin was not the cause of the physical blindness of the man healed by Jesus at the pool of Siloam[33] it certainly was of the Pharisees' spiritual blindness described later in the same chapter.[34] Their problem was a wilful and obstinate closing of their minds and hearts. They did indeed have eyes but did not 'see'[35]. 'Let him who thinks he stands . . . !

---

32   Matthew 13:15; Acts 28:27
33   John 9:3
34   John 9:40,41 and also Matthew 23:19,24
35   Matthew 13:13; Mark 4:12

15 HEARING (and LISTENING)

'Blessed are your ears, for they hear'[1]

So, ears are for hearing! They are the organ of 'hearing'. And, God who 'planted' the ear does he not hear? Hearing, one of the five senses, is that faculty of the body to perceive sound. This 'noblest of our faculties' is intimately linked to our minds. The ability to receive, understand, attend to and process sound is called listening. There is a difference! This is illustrated by a quotation from the letter to the Hebrews.[2] We are to 'pay close attention (listen) to what we have heard (sound)', in this case the voice of God. So, we can hear but 'close our ears'. Nothing wrong with our physical hearing but what happens after that, the listening part, is obstructed, usually intentionally.

The sounds we hear pass through the ear canal (the external auditory meatus) and are then converted by the tympanic membranes of the eardrum into energy that impinges on the three delicate bones of the inner ear. The various components of sound (pitch, rhythm, timbre, tones, sound 'quality'), arriving at the ears as waves, are initially analysed in the fluid filled cochlea, a small coiled instrument located in the inner ear. This acts as a three-dimensional inertial-guidance system, a frequency analyser and acoustical amplifier. It is here that the sound is converted (transduced) into electrical signals by way of receptor receiving cells called 'hair cells'. Deflection of these hair cells leads to a change in electrical voltage of the cell membrane leading to the release of a chemical transmitter. The resultant activation of sensory (afferent) nerve fibres leads to the signal travelling along the auditory nerve to the auditory (somatosensory) area of the cerebral cortex where the information is extracted and 'sorted' so that we perceive what kind of sound it is and where it comes from. It is a mystery why electrical

---

1 Matthew 13:16
2 Hebrews 2:1

signals arriving at this particular area of the somatosensory cortex should be perceived as hearing and not as any of the other senses.

It is interesting that deflection of the hair cells creates a noise of its own, like the 'sound of a soft breeze in the trees'. This indigenous sound, as well as other background noise, the 'white water of auditory stimuli', can be 'turned down' so that we only hear the sounds that interest us, what we want to hear. We thus have the ability to 'switch off', or filter out, irrelevant sounds that do not interest us at the time; we listen to that interesting 'something else' which registers to the exclusion of those (background) sounds that are not relevant at the time and which are the simply made to 'fade'. They 'go in one ear and out the other'!

This process is more difficult as we age. In this 'age impaired' hearing we are unable to focus on relevant information because it is overwhelmed by the interface of distracting information. The result is we move into 'default mode', our brains veer off into their own internal world and we 'day dream'. This is due mainly to a decline in our cerebral nervous connections, probably because of some defect in the brain's chemical messengers.

For those of us with a degree of 'hearing loss' one particular problem encountered is that, if we are surrounded by conflicting noises, the ears are less able to turn off these background sounds. For example, in a room full of noise the swirling sounds bounce off hard surfaces such that, to 'make yourself heard' we need to raise our voice, the so-called Lombard reflex well known to linguists. This problem for the 'hard of hearing' often begins with the loss of those hair cells especially stimulated by the higher frequencies and by some consonants.

'What do you think darling?' says my wife to which my response is something like 'I'm sorry, I "spaced out" and 'missed what you were saying'. It happens quite often! Sadly. But is this a hearing or a listening problem? Think about that last conversation you just had! Who spoke the most? Is not much of our conversation mostly pseudo-dialogue? Did we listen enough to that other person to enable us to really converse? It may sound paradoxical but we must listen if our conversation is to have any value. 'We have two ears and but one mouth that we may listen more and talk less'. To listen is perhaps the greatest service we can perform for another.

Of course, it is not only ageing that limits our ability to hear and hence to listen. Exposure to excessive noise from the use of headphones or from living continuously in an environment of excessive noise, a particular problem for orchestral musicians, especially for those sitting directly in front of the brass or percussion sections!

How can we cope with this form of 'ageing deafness' and rediscover the benefits of better hearing? There have been huge advances in the technology of hearing devices which are now comfortable to wear and near invisible, individually programmed and fitting snugly inside the ear. Or there is 'listen and see', the teletext on television, that 'saviour of the deaf', enabling us to catch up on that inaudible word we missed when the actors were mumbling or those 'asides' when they turned their backs. The other 'add on' advantage of teletext is the humour associated with the, often grotesque, mistakes; pictures for pitches, april for aweful, aisle of man for Isle of Man or 'they came away from that football match with smells (smiles) on their faces'! Recently, there was an account of folk getting off a tour liner on the Scottish east coast and looking forward to seeing 'those mountains and castles but especially Messi' (Nessie!). They should have got off in Barcelona if they had wanted to see the world's number one footballer!

Sadly, as our hearing gets gradually worse we can become more isolated from society and feel more entrapped, foolish and pathetic. 'To every man deaf comes soon or late, a long drawn out introduction to death, down among the deaf men let him lie' wrote Dylan Thomas. There is a moving description of the progress (if that is the right word) into deafness in David Lodge's semi-autobiographical novel *Deaf Sentence*, described by one critic as 'one of the most moving things I have read in a long while'.

Is it possible to hear without hearing, with a totally ineffective hearing apparatus? Beethoven for example, became profoundly deaf at a relatively early age, by his late twenties, perhaps as a result of an untreatable infection. This meant he could not hear, especially his late compositions. Yet, of course he could 'hear' them in his head. We too can 'hear' music in our heads; the memory of familiar music is retained even in its original orchestrated form, and if our voices or hands permit, can be played or sung. Of interest, especially to educationalists (and some politicians) is that musical training, and even quite brief exposure to classical music, enhances other cerebral activities, especially in the still 'plastic brains' of young children. The Mozart effect, so called. There is evidence that mathematical and verbal activities and spatial reasoning are enhanced; perhaps just as important as reading? The orchestral conductor Sir Thomas Beecham once said that if he ever became Prime Minister (it never happened) he would pass a law to the effect that we should listen to the music of Mozart or Haydn each day. One wonders what effect this might have on the reasoning of the general population! Worth trying!

There is a big difference then between simply hearing and really listening. Jonathan Sacks points out that in Hebrew there is no such difference; hearing equals listening, one word for both. James Simpson has an interesting discussion on this in his book *There is a time to . . .* We think predominantly of the words Jesus spoke but Simpson points out that Jesus was a great listener; he listened to Nicodemus with his doubts and questions, to the woman at the well with her account of her tragic family life, to lepers, the blind, the possessed – even to children, much to the amazement of his disciples! He spent so much time just listening to the needs and problems of individuals. Even on the Cross he was still listening – to the dying thief; and listening he acted – 'today you will . . .'[3] In prayer, he listened to his heavenly father. And, he listens to us.

This 'inner hearing' is a question with especial relevance to 'hearing' God's voice, when we read the scriptures for example. God

3   Luke 23:42,43

speaks through the medium of the printed page or, for the blind, through the dots of the Braille bible. How then do we 'hear God' in this way or, even more important, how can we 'listen' to him? Sometimes (and hopefully) by way of the voice of an empowered preacher. However, best of all we listen in the silences, vital to Christian living.

The words for hearing and listening occur well over a thousand times in the bible. Often of course it means hearing with one's ears, the hearing of a sound; Adam and Eve heard, with their ears, the sound of God walking in the Garden, they heard his footsteps! What did that sound like I wonder? They heard his voice.[4] Sarah overheard a conversation between three men (angels) and her husband Abraham,[5] whilst sometimes it was hearing 'the news' passed on by others.[6]

In the New Testament gospels Jesus explained one purpose of his coming was that 'the deaf hear'.[7] Indeed, James Muilenburg maintains that the essential biblical message is contained in the word 'hear' and that the rest is a commentary on this. Of course, there were many people who heard the actual words that Jesus spoke, such as those in the synagogue.[8] they 'heard' a word fulfilled 'in their hearing'. Jesus spoke wonderful words to the disciples again, 'in their hearing'. Felix heard the words spoken to him by Paul[9] about 'faith in Jesus'. So, they and we, hear with our ears; ears are not, of course, the whole body[10] but they are an important part of it.

God too hears and because he is Spirit, without the kind of ears we have. There is a major difference however between God hearing compared to ourselves. God really listens, whether what we say is expressed in words or even when they are unexpressed

---

4 Genesis 3:9,10
5 Genesis 18:10
6 Genesis 29:13
7 Matthew 11:5; Mark 7:37; Luke 7:22
8 Luke 4:21
9 Acts 24:24
10 1 Corinthians 12:17

and 'spoken' in the silence of our own hearts. God is attentive to our voice, he hears us 'from heaven when we call',[11] he listens. God really listens. The psalmist emphasises that God hears our cry,[12] our call.[13] God says 'because you prayed I heard you'.[14] He hears our individual prayers,[15] the prayers of the needy, the orphans and widows[16] but especially the prayers of his beloved Son.[17]

Because God is attentive to our voice in prayer he not only listens but also responds. He answers; the listening is followed by 'doing', it results in action, in helping.[18] It is because we can have this assurance that God hears us and responds that we have confidence; access into his presence bringing our needs to him. We 'have a great High Priest'[19] who is able to take our feeble, inadequate prayers and present them, in his own words, to the Father. It is the voice of the Lord Jesus[20] and the voice of the Holy Spirit who intercede on our behalf.[21] The Son and the Spirit, those perfect intercessors, are praying for us to the Father who hears, listens and acts!

As we have seen there is a huge difference between hearing and listening. Jesus told a story about hearing and listening[22] ending with the words (paraphrased as) 'anyone with ears to hear (most of us) should listen and understand'. This 'parable of the listeners' deals with the reception of God's word by different kinds of listeners. There are those who fail to take it in at all, it 'goes in one ear and out of the other'; that word is 'swept away'; it is as though it was never spoken or heard at all. Other 'listeners' have so many concerns with day to day things that the word is choked before it

---

11 2 Chronicles 7:14,15
12 Psalm 145:19
13 Psalm 4:3
14 2 Kings 19:20; 20:5; 2 Chronicles 34:27
15 Judges 13:9; 1 Kings 17:22; 2 Chronicles 30:20
16 Exodus 22:22,23
17 John 11:41,42; Hebrews 5:7
18 Isaiah 49:8; 2 Corinthians 6:2
19 Hebrews 4:14
20 Romans 8:34
21 Romans 8:26,27
22 Matthew 13:3–9

can have any influence their lives; it may be thought about but it has no lasting impact. The 'weeds' leave no room for God's word. The word is hindered, rejected, resisted; it becomes 'an offence'.[23] However, there are some who do receive it, welcome it, and who listen and absorb what God is saying. The key phrase is 'take root' in 'good soil' with all that implies for growth and fruitfulness. We become 'doers of that word' and not simply hearers.[24]

When we really listen to what someone is saying to us there is an immediate and appropriate response, there is dialogue and then there is action. So, part of our response to what we hear from God is to respond back to God in conversation. 'What does this mean for me Lord? Why are you telling me this today and how do you want me to respond? What are my instructions for today?' If human words have power when they are received, and believed by receptive and attentive hearers (I think for example of the wartime speeches and oratory of Winston Churchill or of the great preachers of past years) how much more in its effect is the mighty and powerful word of God, a word which convicts, inspires, comforts, guides, edifies and brings peace? God's word, read or preached upon is to be received with gladness and faith. As Jesus himself said 'he who has ears let him (really) hear'!

At the end of each of the letters to the seven churches in Revelation (chapters 2 and 3) these words come again – 'he who has an ear let him hear' what the Spirit is saying. We are to be, as the apostle James says[25] 'quick to hear'. This then means to pay close undivided attention to what we hear from God, to take these words into our minds, to let them 'sink in' and keep them there, to listen with action, with obedience. The lovely old English word 'hearken' has this idea of responding, acting on, giving audience to and obeying one with authority.[26] It is an attentive exercise which leads to understanding (knowledge) and agreement.

---

23 Mark 6:3; John 6:66
24 James 1:22
25 James 1:19
26 Acts 2;14; James 2:5 (AV)

16 TOUCH

*'Put (touch with) your finger here . . . do not disbelieve
but believe'[1]*
'His touch has still its ancient power'

Touch is one of the five special senses; together with seeing, hearing, taste and smell, they are our links with the world outside us. Sensors that respond to touch 'sense' changes in the external environment by coming into contact with it. Such receptors are small, incongruous seed-like structures mounted on a mobile surface, the skin. This enables us to choose how and when they can be stimulated; instead of waiting for the world to touch us we can reach out and touch it whenever we choose. It is exploration, awareness of our outside physical world. To 'feel' means to search, to examine, to handle, by means of the physical sensation of 'touch' the various objects within our reach. For example, the woman Eve[2] reminds the serpent that God had said that both she and Adam were not even to 'touch' the fruit of the tree in the midst of the garden, let alone eat it. Jacob's thigh was touched by the 'man' at Jabbok[3] and in the New Testament there are many examples of Jesus physically touching, with his hands, individuals with bodily disabilities, the blind, the sick, the deaf, the unclean, even the dead in order to heal and restore.

The physiology of touch is a somatic sensation involving very small, inconspicuous 'receptors', special anatomical structures, invisible to the naked eye and present everywhere throughout the body, both 'inside' and out. One of the several types of skin end-organ is the Pacinian corpuscle that looks a little like an oval shaped onion. These wonderful sensors in our skin have a remarkable

---

1   John 20:27
2   Genesis 3:3
3   Genesis 32:25,32

ability to distinguish between different surfaces, hard from soft, wood from plastic, even between different types of fabric. I have often watched in wonder my mother-in-law 'reading' with her fingers; from middle age, when she was losing her sight, she learnt braille, small projections on paper the position of which indicated different letters of the alphabet.

Touch then is a sensory phenomenon but it is not simply passive; it has a motor component as well. Action (for example, stroking, gripping) is an important response to what we feel. Touch then is active; we can 'feel' the coins in our pockets by their shape and whether or not they have ridges. As I write, fountain pen in hand (this is one of several initial drafts of this chapter on touch!) I can 'feel' the pen between my thumb and the first two fingers of my right hand, guiding the pen across the paper, depending upon the pressure felt by the touch receptors in the skin. The resultant skeletal muscles of my hand then guide the pen to produce the letters I am looking for.

Of course, sight too is involved in this process; unlike when I play the piano, feeling the notes without looking at them. The really good pianist has a good sense of 'touch', feeling, exploring the keys (through the receptors at the tips of the fingers), passing the information to the brain through the appropriate sensory nerves (what the great English physiologist Sir Charles Sherrington called the 'way in' to the brain) and then responding by varying the intensity of pressure on the keys, through 'motor' nerves to the muscles of the hand. The intensity of this nerve traffic, the 'way out' from the brain, determines the extent of the pressure on the piano keys. Sight, once the music has been learnt is now of little, if any, importance. In contrast, when I am writing with my pen I need to see what has been written. If I were to close my eyes my handwriting would be even more indecipherable than it is with my eyes open!

Fingers are wonderful! Indeed, Isaac Newton once said that 'the thumb alone would convince me of the existence of God'! Think of the way that the hand is designed, with the thumb at ninety degrees to the fingers. This enables us to grip and guide a pen (the precision grip), to hold firmly on to the handlebars of a bicycle (the power grip) and to pick up and carry a shopping bag with only the fingers (the 'hanging grip'). Can other parts of the body take over from the hands and fingers? For years now we have received cards and calendars from a group of disabled painters devoid of the use of their hands. They continue to paint effectively with the brush held in their mouths or even with their toes. These paintings are quite amazing!

Through touch then we explore the outside world nearest to us, apprehending the local environment. It is a form of communing with the world that confronts us. We can reach out to it. This exploration of the environment through touch begins early in life, even in the developing foetus. Certainly, in young babies it is how they first explore their environment, including their own bodies, particularly with their lips, mouth and fingers. It is, at this stage in their life, the most important of the senses. Babies with a touch deficiency can become disabled developmentally. At the other end of the life cycle these touch sensors are the last of the sense organs to leave us at the end of life. Hence the importance to the dying of holding and stroking the hand as they leave this present world.

Following mechanical stimulation of these touch receptors a stream of nerve impulses passes along the appropriate peripheral nerve fibres, the intensity of stimulation being mirrored by the frequency of these nerve impulses. Such sensory nerve fibres are on their 'way in', to a region of the brain called the somatosensory cortex which we have come across in previous chapters when dealing with sight and hearing. The largest part of the region of the cortex concerned with touch are those arising from sensors in the index fingers and the lips. These ceaselessly inform the brain about what is happening in the environment. We feel with our minds! There is no human activity, art, music, cooking, writing, that does not initially rely on 'touch'. On the body surfaces these receptors are present in particularly large numbers on the fingertips, lips, tongue and on the sexual organs.

It is debatable whether these touch receptors (better called sensors) are different from those associated with pressure and vibration but they are certainly distinct from those which sense heat, cold and pain. This has been demonstrated by physiologists using stiff bristles to stimulate the touch receptors; there are however areas of the skin where the bristle cannot be felt but it can be shown, when using a fine metal probe capable of being heated and placed at these same points, that these same areas of skin are sensitive to heat but not to pressure. Another example of this differentiation between skin pressure and heat sensors is when a limb 'goes to sleep'. The sensation to touch is lost but not that to heat. In a medical condition known as syringomelia the patient retains the sense of touch but loses an appreciation of hot and cold.

It is possible to estimate the threshold of different parts of the body surface to mechanical stimulation and touch. The most sensitive are the lips and the tips of the fingers. Less sensitive is the skin of the palms of the hands, the toes and the soles of the feet. Even less sensitive to touch is the skin overlying the chest, shoulders and abdomen. These differences depend upon the number and distribution of the sensors on the skin surface and how close they are to each other, so called spatial resolution.

Similar receptors are present also within the body. In voluntary muscles these sensors (called proprioceptors) are particularly sensitive to stretch. They are also present in ligaments and tendons. Similar sensors are found within the walls of certain blood vessels, for example in the aortic arch, where they respond mainly to changes in pressure (baroceptors) or to in the chemical composition of the blood (chemoreceptors). Such sensors found within the body are termed 'enteroceptors' as opposed to those on the surfaces which are called exteroceptors.

In the Old Testament the word used for touch and feel (and reach) is used about a hundred and fifty times. There are things that are forbidden to touch, objects rather than people, like the tree of knowledge in the garden of Eden[4] or the 'unclean' things in Leviticus. It was forbidden to touch the 'holy' ark and, as it was brought 'home' following its capture by the Philistines, from Gibeah to the city of David, Uzzah inadvertently touched it and died 'by the hand of the Lord'.[5] Abimelech was forbidden to 'touch' sexually Sarah, the wife of Abraham.[6] In the New Testament a similar word is translated as 'fasten', 'lay hold of' and is used, for example, in the letter to the Corinthians of carnal intercourse with a woman[7] and of fellowship with unbelievers.[8] The command is 'do not touch'.

Jesus often used touch with his fingers to heal, touching to restore physical health. On some occasions this healing was sometimes through an intermediate such as garments[9] or a bier[10] but was most commonly by direct touch. The instances are numerous. The blind,[11] the deaf and dumb (often with a combination of touch and spittle),[12] the leprous,[13] a man with dropsy, possibly a form of cardiac failure,[14] a woman bent double[15] and even the dead[16] were touched with the fingers of Jesus. Such healing often also involved spiritual healing, for example peace and forgiveness. In the case of Thomas it led to belief, to faith.[17] This is the biblical rationale and impetus for Christian medical missions.

So, there is an emotional and spiritual component to 'touch' especially when the touch is from God. For example, it can

---

4   Genesis 3:3
5   2 Samuel 6:4-7
6   Genesis 20:6
7   1 Corinthians 7:1
8   2 Corinthians 6:17
9   Mark 5:25-34; 6:56
10 Luke 7:14
11 Matthew 9:29; 20:34, Mark 8:22
12 Mark 7:31-35
13 Matthew 8:3; Mark 1:41; Luke 5:13
14 Luke 14:2,4
15 Luke 13:11-13
16 Matthew 9:25; Mark 5:41; Luke 8:54
17 John 20:27, 28

concern an ability to speak for God ('He has touched my lips').[18] Often it refers to receiving the Holy Spirit. Saul,[19] the Samaritans[20] and the Ephesians[21] were 'touched' by the Spirit. And in prayer, two people agreeing ('touching anything') on what they ask for, have a special promise, 'it shall be done'.[22] In prayer and in spiritual experience the touch of the Lord, as the hymn writer put it, 'still has ancient power'.

There is considerable overlap (called 'crosstalk') between touching and seeing. Indeed, when people look at an area of their bodies which is being touched, there is greater activity in that area of the somatosensory cortex dealing with this sensation than when that area is touched but not looked at. The reverse is also true. Giving people both a touch and a visual stimulus at the same time enhances activity in the visual sensory cortex. There are examples of this in scripture. Jesus both 'touched and saw' and invited others to do the same. The disciples were invited to touch him after the resurrection[23] but contrast his word to Mary 'touch me not', meaning 'do not cling'.[24] On the other hand Thomas, in response to his declaration 'unless I see and put (touch) my fingers in the print of the nails',[25] was invited to both 'touch (put) and see', leading to belief. And that touch has 'still its ancient power'!

---

18 Isaiah 6:7; Jeremiah 1:9; Daniel 10:16
19 Paul; Acts 9:12,17
20 Acts 8:17-19
21 Acts 19:6
22 Matthew 18:19
23 Luke 24:39
24 John20:17
25 John 20:25

17 TASTE

'Taste and see that the Lord is good'[1]

When we eat or drink we perceive a sensation we call 'taste'. There is a great value in 'savouring', enjoying both the taste and texture of what we eat and drink, drawing out every possible bit of flavour. A pleasurable experience! The cells responsible for such sensations are scattered around the surface of the tongue and the soft palate of the mouth and, as food is moved around the mouth these taste buds are stimulated. These 'buds', which are shaped like a very small onion, contain a variable number (from about 200 to 20,000) of gustatory receptors. On stimulation of these receptors by chemical substances from food and drink dissolved in saliva, which acts as both a solvent for these substances and also a means of 'transporting' these substances to the taste buds. The sensation message is then relayed to the 'taste' area of the cerebral cortex. This area of the brain enables us to decide and remember what foods we enjoy. The sensation of taste is closely linked with that of smell (olfaction) as becomes clear when the nose is blocked, for example, as a result of a common cold, when the sense of taste is much reduced.

We usually categorise the sensation of taste receptors, situated in different areas of the tongue, into five 'modalities' – salt, sour, sweet, bitter and umami, from the Japanese for good (*umai*) and taste (*mi*). The latter is responsible for our appreciation of the ability to savour foods with such different flavours, cheese from mushrooms, pineapple, cucumber etc. Individual variations in taste perception and food appreciation is due to the number and location within the mouth of these gustatory receptor cells but there is also a genetic and gender component, for example the often unexplainable desire for certain foods during pregnancy.

---

1 Psalm 34:8

Taste cells have a relatively short lifespan, of the order of ten or so days; they are replaced from epithelial stem cells. There are other receptors in the mouth which respond to differences in temperature and texture (smoothness) which also modify the sense of 'taste'. Taste then enables us to distinguish between, and appreciate, the foods we eat making dining so pleasurable. We inhabit our very own taste world! Spare a thought then for those unfortunates unable to distinguish between the endless varieties of the foods we eat, or even perhaps unable, for some reason, to taste at all.

But what is the primary function of the sensation of taste? First, exploration. It is a call to explore and, if we like that particular food, to swallow and then digest. Have you ever, we might be asked, tasted this? This was a question often asked of us during the years we spent in Africa! The fiery assault on the tongue of those hot peppers which, if accidentally spilt, could burn a hole in the tablecloth or even in the table itself! Then, for wine tasters, those marked differences in the taste of wine depending on the type of grape and the location where grown, with the resultant variations in acidity, dryness, sweetness and the seemingly endless additional flavours apparently resembling peach, melon, nuts, gooseberries, mango or honeysuckle.

Second, the sensation of taste is concerned with our protection. There are dangers of putting things into our mouths, as those with young children know only too well. With intelligence and teaching we learn to reject anything that seems suspect; our sense of taste saves us from the almost irreversible act of swallowing. The fact that we have a variety of bitter taste receptors is a device for protecting very young children from poisoning themselves. The nausea and aversion to certain foods during pregnancy, especially in the early stages, is another example of the protective role of our taste buds by reducing the exposure to the foetus of naturally occurring toxins, not necessary damaging to the adult.

Third, the sense of taste is not, of course, the end of the process of digestion. It is preparatory. It 'leads to' swallowing and ingestion. Babies love milk, after that exploratory taste.

They can often distinguish between breast and formulated milk before making the decision to swallow. The introduction, at the right stage, of 'solids' is also proceeded by taste appreciation; the youngster might like one food and prefer another and this on the basis of taste. This ability to distinguish between foods becomes more and more comprehensive and pleasing up to adulthood, but then sadly is often lost in 'old age'.

How does this help us in an understanding of taste in scripture? Our word above from Psalm 34:8 to 'taste and see' is clearly exploratory. It was also a question that Paul asked the church in Galatia;[2] they had 'transferred their allegiance', from him who had called them in the grace of Christ, to another 'gospel'. They had begun with Christ, had 'tasted him' but that taste had lost its sweetness; they no longer imbibed. All faith begins with exploration and, as in science, with a question – or more than one! How much is missed, both in religion and science, because of not being prepared for that initial exploration, that first 'taste'. To taste Christ, his person and his benefits leads to the, often dramatic, discovery that having first tasted we find that he is indeed 'gracious'.[3] Then God's word becomes sweet to us, like honey.[4] So, we are first to hear God's word; 'the ear tests words as the palate tastes food' and we are to 'chose what is right and good'. We do not, if we are wise, like the tea or wine taster, taste and then spit it out.

The author to the letter to the Hebrews[5] speaks of those who have 'tasted of the free heavenly gift' and have 'tasted' ('knew from experience' GNV) the goodness of the word of God'. This heavenly gift is Jesus himself; when Jesus talked to the Samaritan woman at the well he identified himself as the 'gift of God'[6] whilst the gift of the Holy Spirit[7] of grace and of righteousness are all associated

2   Galatians 1:6
3   1 Peter 2:3
4   Psalm 119:103
5   Hebrews 6:4,5
6   John 4:10
7   Acts 2:33

with the gift of Jesus himself. To taste means the enjoyment of receiving these gifts, the whole sum of spiritual blessings, for the nourishment of our lives which comes from the taste and the 'swallowing' of them making them our own.

Is it possible then to lose this sense of taste? This seems to be the context of the remainder of Hebrews 6, a warning of apostasy, of falling away. It is certainly possible physically; Barzillai, at eighty, complained that he could no longer taste food or drink.[8] Sadly, this can also be true spiritually. Such folk are then said to be 'tasteless', tepid (neither hot nor cold) and thus 'spewn' (spat) out of the Lord's mouth.[9] Jesus told a parable about this. Sadly it is also possible, despite the psalmist's experience[10] to lose a taste for God's word. This is often the beginning of a spiritual downward slide. We need a sensitive and trained appreciation of the pleasures and delights of God's word which comes from a regular tasting process.

The other scriptural reference to 'taste' comes in a somewhat different context. In Jeremiah[11] the criticism of Moab was that it was 'at ease', 'settled on the lees'. The reference is to wine making; if allowed to settle too long (on the lees) without being agitated and poured from one vessel to another (decanted) it loses its pungency and flavour; one is left with a bitter taste.

So, how sensitive are our spiritual taste buds? To taste is to explore, investigate, experience, savour and to enjoy both the Lord himself and his word, to draw out every possible bit of flavour with that 'after taste' still in our mouths so that 'his taste remains in him' and 'his scent (aroma) is unchanged'. Maybe this was in Paul's mind when he wrote that passage about carrying always with us the aroma and the 'taste' of Christ.[12]

---

8   2 Samuel 19:34,35
9   Revelation 3:16
10   Psalm 119:103
11   Jeremiah 48:11
12   2 Corinthians 2:14-16

18 SMELL (Olfaction)
'For we are an aroma of Christ to God'[1]

The least intellectual of the senses, a skill of minor importance, or the most intimate way of interacting with the external environment? Scripture has much to tell us about smell, fragrance and odours. But again, let us begin with a definition. Smell is the faculty of perceiving odours, by inhalation, in order to ascertain, detect and discern the properties of a substance having an effect on the nasal mucosa. Recognizable, because smell so often brings back the past to mind and with it associated discernment, judgement and choice.

Smells can be pleasant (fragrant, sweet-smelling, odoriferous) or decidedly unpleasant (malodorous, foul, fetid, offensive, putrid). Interestingly there are more words to describe an unpleasant smell than a pleasant one. Words like stench, stink, reek and pong. The mechanisms through which we detect odours involve the interaction between the odoriferous molecule and the chemoreceptor cells situated at the back and top of the air passage in the nose.

This area is small in humans, about the size of a postage stamp, yet in this small area there are about 20 million of these receptor cells, which are, in fact, neurones (nerve cells). In other animals, dogs for example, this area is much larger and the sense of smell much more pronounced, giving them the ability to detect by sniffing, for example drugs and explosives. The olfactory mucous membrane is thus the place in the body where the nervous system is closest to the external world. This mucosa is rich in blood vessels with 'vascular lakes' similar to those found in erectile tissue elsewhere in the body.

How complex organic chemicals trigger the particular receptors involved is only partially known. Perhaps they dissolve

---
1 2 Corinthians 2:15

(or puncture?) the receptor protein molecules imbedded, as a mosaic, in the lipid double layer of the mucosa. These receptors are continually being replaced every few weeks which makes the link between the detection of an odour and memory all the more astonishing and wonderful. These receptors are highly sophisticated and sensitive, able to identify and distinguish between thousands of different odours, some in the one part in a billion range. Garlic, for example, can be detected in a concentration of less than 500pg/litre of air! This sensitivity is amazing with the ability to distinguish between two different odours from substances differing by just a single molecule.

The messages from the receptors are then taken, via millions of the olfactory nerve endings, to a structure called the olfactory bulb and, by way of the first (olfactory) cranial nerve, to the lower brain, to an area known as the orbitofrontal cortex. This area of the brain is closely linked with other areas which are associated with mood, memory and decision making.

Smell has the unique ability to trigger long-term childhood memories. The Times columnist Caitlin Moran has written of her memories of her mother's perfume, the smell of moss and wood when climbing trees, and of the pencil shavings at the bottom of her school bag. Other childhood memories triggered by scent which come to mind include the smell of the coal tar of roads in hot weather, of seaweed and freshly mown grass, of autumn bonfires, of plasticine, lavender, freshly washed hair, football boots newly cleaned and, for the author, a father's tobacco smoke and that cowshed left for weeks to be cleaned! Such smells, when they reoccur, take us back often over many years to when we were young, with all their associations of places and people. Especially poignant when the reminders are of loved ones who have died. Marcel Proust once wrote 'after the people are dead the smell and taste of things remain poised a long time, the immense edifice of memory'. These odours live on, never changing.

Odours are difficult to describe in words. Certainly, it is possible to distinguish between pleasant and unpleasant smells and 'scale' them accordingly but one has to resort to phrases such as 'it is like' an object we can see and feel or a condition (burnt, stale, rotten, mouldy, old socks). Thus, the scent of a Chardonnay can be described as 'like' a complex of nuts, butter, toast, apple and lemon whilst Semillon is 'like' butterscotch, honeysuckle and mango. Perfume is even more difficult to describe.

There is a close relation between smell and sexual and social attractiveness; evaluation of smell, it is said, is apparently as important as facial gestures or talk. In rural Austria at one time girls kept a slice of apple in their armpits and 'presented' them to the swain of their choice at the end of an evening of dancing with the hope that they were 'turned on' by the smell. Certainly, glands which abound in the face, nipples, scrotum and the pubic region secrete odourless oily substances which are then broken down by microorganisms, living around the hair follicles of the 'axillary jungle', to musky smelling substances. These, once airborne, can influence mood behaviour and libido and can be emotionally evocative. Yet such odours evoke a desire, a yearning seldom fulfilled. In women, such 'pheromones' (from the word meaning to transfer and then excite) vary during the phases of the menstrual cycle and are 'more pleasant' during the fertile phase of the cycle, and during breast feeding, than elsewhere in the cycle. Such odours on clothing can last for days.

In the Song of Solomon fragrances 'colour' much of the relationship between Solomon and his Shulamite bride. Solomon speaks that 'the fragrance of your oils (natural?} are better then all kinds of spices',[2] that her breath is 'like' apples and her mouth 'like the best wine'. He himself 'came up from the wilderness like columns of smoke perfumed with myrrh and frankincense'.[3] Elsewhere, at table, the bride says that 'my perfume gave forth its fragrance', perhaps from a pouch of perfume worn around the neck. Indeed, the universal use of costly oils and perfumes for health and beauty were commonplace in domestic life,

2 Song of Solomon 4:10
3 Song of Solomon 3:6

when anointing the body contributed to comfort in a hot environment. It was common courtesy, as we will see from incidents in the gospels of Mark and John, for guests to be so anointed as a token of welcome or before leaving home for 'entertainments'. These perfumes were often contained in jars made of porcelain or alabaster. So strong can be the odour from perfume that an alabaster jar found in Alnwick Castle in Northumberland, retained its scent after two to three thousand years!

Even today smell can be used as a diagnostic instrument; the powerful smell from a gangrenous limb or, in patients with diabetes mellitus, the degradation products of fat, ketone bodies, gives to urine an odour of acetone, and to the breath a not unpleasant smell of apples. Saint Jerome was said to be able to detect avariciousness, loose morals and signs of female sexual misconduct from the 'smell' of the individual; or the sweet perfume of celestial bliss! The saints of old were often perceptibly odorous which everyone could confirm with the nose because of the wonderful aroma of their clothes. Modesty and virtue oozed from every pore! An odour of sanctity. Later this phrase 'odour of sanctity' was used in a quite different sense, for example that of 'the odious Obadiah Slope' (so appropriately named!) in the Barchester novels of Anthony Trollope.

In scripture we read of 'the smell of the field',[4] of burning and of fire[5] and of battle.[6] It also talks of the lethal power of bad, unclean, foul smells. The river Nile 'stank' from the excrement and decomposition of animals[7] whilst in Isaiah[8] God likened his people to vines that only produced wild grapes. And this despite all he had done for them. One translation of the word 'wild' is 'stinky', mouldy.

---

4   Genesis 27:27
5   Daniel 3:27
6   Job 39:25
7   Exodus 8:14
8   Isaiah 5:2,4

Such oppressive smells continue to harass and discourage because they are so difficult to remove. Our cities in times past must have been particularly filthy and odorous, the sewage of mediaeval cities (and some cities with open sewers in Africa today), the pong of revolutionary Paris (the tanneries and the rotting flesh of pigs). In an interesting TV programme a while ago on the 'real smell of history' (together with appropriate scratch cards!) comment was made about the pervading stench of human and animal excrement in ancient Rome, the bad breath of the first Queen Elizabeth, the smell of rotting fish in Georgian England and the slinging of the slimy contents of chamber pots from upstairs windows, depicted by William Hogarth in 1736 in his cartoon 'Night'. There is a wonderful Scottish word – mingin, to aptly describe a degree of dirt upon one's person, a less than floral odour. As in 'Ye's a fair mingin the day, walkin a that manky glaur intae ma clean flair'.

But let us return to those pleasant fragrancies recorded in Scripture! Mark places such a spontaneous act of love[9] between two descriptions of acts of hatred, the plot to kill Jesus by the chief priests and scribes and Judas' betrayal. We are told that the ointment of nard (from the spikenard plant) was both pure (genuine), costly – because of the transport costs involved in 'many camel miles' – and precious. Perhaps the alabaster jar of ointment was a family heirloom passed down from her mother. The jar itself was broken to release the perfume, a lavish act of extravagance. The fragrance then 'filled the whole house' stimulating those olfactory nerve endings. That fragrance would always be associated with this act of love and indeed, would, in the future, recall the presence of the Lord himself. There is a similar account in John's gospel (chapter 12) of such an act of love. This took place in the Bethany home in of Lazarus and his two sisters. Here, it is Mary who took a whole pound of expensive perfume and anointed Jesus' feet. Both of these

---

9 Mark 14:3,4

women (if they are indeed two separate incidents) showed Jesus the highest honour, regardless of expense and indifferent to the criticism of those around them. Indeed, this fragrance speaks of Christ Himself, the 'holy perfume of the divine nature'. Thus, Paul in Ephesians[10] writes that 'Christ loved us and gave himself as a fragrant offering[11] and sacrifice to God'. Here there is a reminder of the Old Testament sacrifices when the pleasing aroma from them went up to God.[12]

Just as Christ by his life and sacrifice was 'a fragrant offering' to God so we too are to be to God a fragrance, the aroma of Christ himself.[13] And, not only to God but to the world. We Christians are to be the 'unmistakable scent' of Christ, discernible alike to those who are being saved ('a fresh fragrance of life itself') and to those heading for death (the very 'smell of doom' – Phillips). Our Christian lives are to create a crisis for those we meet, confirming ('from life to life') those who belong to Christ but also as a warning to those, who at that time are lost.

This is an awesome responsibility for those of us who live as Christians. As Paul explains, only Christ is sufficient for these things. We are to leave behind us an 'aroma' of Christ; the probable picture here is that of a Roman procession during which incense was burning. The aroma was 'left behind' when the procession moved on. Here again that close link of smell with memory. Such a link is again illustrated in the story of Peter's re-commissioning[14] after his denial of Christ in the Temple courtyard.[15] Was it that smell of the charcoal fire that brought back to Peter's mind his denial and thus prepared him to receive forgiveness and future service?

The nerve endings at the back of the nose concerned with the sense of smell have another unique property. They are the

10 Ephesians 5:2
11 Crushed, Isaiah 53:10
12 Exodus 29: 18,25,41
13 2 Corinthians 2:14-17
14 John 21:15-19
15 John 18:18 and 21:9

only part of the nervous system that is able to spontaneously regenerate, which they do throughout our lives. This is perhaps because they are directly exposed to, and damaged by, the pollution and infections in the atmosphere – an important first line of defence. This property has been utilised in a rather exciting way. Professor Geoffrey Raisman at University College in London has used cultures of these cells to repair the damage which occurs when the nerves within the spinal cord have been severed. This is achieved by using these 'nasal cells' to form a bridge between the ends of the severed fibres. There are trials underway to determine if this technique can be used to repair spinal injury in patients.

19 PUTTING IT ALL TOGETHER
'Ow de body' - one body many parts

What we have looked at in the preceding pages are some of the individual activities of the whole body. What we now think about is how these activities are integrated within that body. This is a little like recent scientific approaches to the physical body. For example, there has been much emphasis in molecular biology on the reductionist 'genes eye view' of life, breaking down living systems into their smallest components. The Oxford physiologist Dennis Noble in his book *The Music of Life*[1] has argued eloquently for the need to 're-assemble the organism' – in this case the whole body. 'Humpty Dumpty has been smashed into billions of fragments; he needs to be put together again'.

The kind of elementary physiology outlined in the present book is, of course, not that reductionist and anyway there was a particular purpose in mind in writing it, looking at the words describing those activities of the body that contribute to our everyday lives and which also occur in the Bible. However, we need now finally to think about the body as a whole rather than of its constituent parts. Even Noble himself only goes half way; he moves from the very small (genes, molecules) to, for the most part, the still quite small (isolated cardiac muscle). As the Scottish one-time winner of the Nobel Prize for Physiology and Medicine, the late Sir James Black was always keen to emphasise, we need to move from dealing with individual (and in most scientific studies isolated) organ systems to the so well integrated 'whole body'. We are more than the 'sum of our parts'. Let us then, in this final chapter, seek to 'put the body together again'. Not so easy! As the

---

1   Noble, D. *The Music of Life. Biology Beyond Genes*, Oxford University Press, 2006

psalmist said[2] we are 'formed and knitted together'. No dropped stitches!

Completeness

The body is 'one' – one entity, as Paul noted in his letter to the church in Corinth,[3] the various parts of the body are incomplete by themselves; they need one another. We are not all heart or all ears or eyes or nostrils. These parts all belong together. Only together are they complete.

Of course, we know now that some isolated organ systems can exist outside the body. It is possible, for example, that hearts isolated from the body, provided they are bathed in a suitable artificial blood solution and well oxygenated, can be kept beating and 'alive' for many hours. The same is true for smooth muscle isolated from the digestive or urinary tracts. Such preparations are the 'bread and butter' of many working physiologists and pharmacologists. It is also true that such studies have told us much about how these respond in the intact body. But individually they do not comprise 'us'. They remain 'parts'. Clearly too, organs removed from the body of the donor and ready for transplantation (heart, lungs, liver, kidney) are kept alive under certain highly critical conditions (cold, perhaps now, oxygenated) sometimes for a considerable time before use.

Not all of these individual 'parts' are essential for life. We can exist, many do, without the ability to hear, see, smell or walk, but no-one is alive without a heart, a circulation, lungs, a digestive tract or especially a brain. These are the 'essential' organs. However, for living as we were originally made to be we need each 'part'. It is only together that we are complete. 'All the members of the body (put together) are one' can refer to the physical body as well as to the church. Of course, this does not mean that the functions of each part are the same. No 'member' can perform another's part. Every 'part' is needed. If one part

---

2 Psalm 139:13
3 1 Corinthians 12:12-25

of the body is deprived, injured, left out, then the whole body suffers. It is incomplete.

This theme of completeness was taken up in Paul's illustration of the church of Jesus as his body, a body of people that belong to him. So, the church, despite its many sad divisions, is one - 'you were called in **one body**'.[4] It is true that it has many physical individual members, today more than ever, but the phrase[5] '**all** the members, although many, are **one body**' speaks of a spiritual unity that Jesus earnestly desired and prayed for.[6] And, one day that prayer will be answered.

Activity

The body is continually active. Like God himself it never sleeps. We may, but our body does not. Our bodies are working around the clock. All the time our cells are being fed, they are metabolising, they are excreting, because they are living, active. So it is with the body of Christ. Every moment someone, somewhere in the world, is worshipping, praying, learning, listening to God, speaking to God. The song, as the hymn says, 'goes round the world that Jesus Christ is Lord'. It never stops. Neither do we.

Integration

The body is marvellously 'arranged'; it is integrated, all the parts are wonderfully interconnected. Paul, speaking about the physical body talks about its composition – 'God has so composed the body'.[7] That is the way God 'arranged' it. Each part dependent on another. An obvious example is the 'part' we call the circulation (see chapter 9). The transport of oxygen, crucial for the life of every cell in the body, depends on the heart working as a pump, on the blood, the lungs and on the nervous connections between them. Every individual cell is critically dependent on the flowing

---

4   Colossians 3:15; 4:4-6
5   1 Corinthians 12:12
6   John 17:21
7   1 Corinthians 12:24 (ESV)

blood to cart away the rubbish they produce. These, and all the other activities of the body, are well coordinated by the brain. They belong together.

The illustration of the body, both physical and spiritual, as an orchestra is an appropriate one. Each 'member', from the leader of the first violin section to the second (or third) bassoon is essential to the performance as a whole. At a recent rehearsal by a well-known symphony orchestra, I was interested to notice that the player of the E flat clarinet had just three notes to play during the whole two-hour rehearsal. But how essential those three notes turned out to be! Without it that particular piece would have made little sense. Perhaps, for the rest of the time he was reading a novel perched on his music stand. Not unknown. I once noticed this happening during an actual performance! Each orchestral part, and the player of that part, is essential to the whole. There is harmony. A performance would be incomplete if say, the viola section went on strike. Unless there was no part for them to play in that particular musical score. And, does the orchestra even need a conductor? Many orchestras play without one. Or do they even need the music score in front of them? One orchestra plays music from memory. Usual for concerto soloists but some feat for a whole orchestra!

As I watch an orchestra perform I often wonder about the role of the conductor. Is it a better performance I wonder, if the conductor is also the composer of the music being played because, in a special way, the music is 'inside him'; that is where it came from. All the classical composers (Haydn, Mozart, Beethoven) conducted their own music and even recordings seem fresher when the composer was present or conducting his own work. Listen, for example, to the recordings of how Elgar or Vaughan Williams or Britten conduct the music that originated from them.

So, that word 'composed' is appropriate. It comes in

scripture where it refers to both the human physical body[8] and the church as the body of Christ. We could say of the body as we could of all great music, 'well composed'. And, we could say of both kinds of body God has 'composed', 'tempered together', moderated, 'adjusted' (Calvin), 'harmonised' (Phillips). God is 'in control'. As David Prior[9] has pointed out, it is God who has 'appointed', 'assigned', 'arranged', 'composed'. True both of our physical body and the church. Both marvellously made!

---

8 Psalm 139:15 (translation by Pamela Greenberg, *The Complete Psalms*, New York, Bloomsburg, 2010)

9 Prior, D. *The Message of 1 Corinthians*, Leicester, Inter Varsity Press, 1985

TRAVELLING ON – FURTHER READING

For any reader wishing to 'travel further' into the wonders of the human body here are some suggestions:

The Body

Ed. Blakemore, C. and Jennett, S., *The Oxford Companion to the Body,* Oxford University Press, 2001. (A kind of physiologist's bible, huge and comprehensive.)

Ewing, W.A., *Inside Information – Imaging the Human Body,* London, Thames and Hudson, 1996. (Incredible photographs of the 'inside'.)

Miller, J., *The Body in Question,* London, Thames and Hudson, 1978.

Ackerman, J., *A Day in the Life of your Body,* Boston, Houghton Mifflin, 2007. (Quite simply, brilliant!)

Brand, P. and Yancey, P., *Fearfully and Wonderfully Made,* London, Hodder and Stoughton, 1981.

Brand, P. and Yancey, P., *In His Image.* London, Hodder and Stoughton,1984. (Both of these books are classics, never surpassed.)

Francis, G., *Adventures in Human Being,* London, Welcome Collection, 2015.

Individual Chapters

Speakman, C., *Walk! A Celebration of Striding Out,* Ilkley, Great Northern Books, 2011.

Burton, A.C., *Physiology and Biophysics of the Circulation,* Chicago, Year Book Medical, 1966.

Halpern, S., *Can't Remember What I Forgot – The Good News from the Front Line of Memory Research,* New York, Harmony Books, 2008.

Price, J., *The Woman Who Can't Forget,* New York, Simon and Schuster, 2008.

Gawande, A., *Being Mortal,* London, Profile Books, 2015. (Superb!)

Webber, A., *Life Later On – Older People and the Church,* London, SPCK, 1990.

Tournier, P., *Learning to Grow Old,* London, SCM Press, 1972.

Gonzalez-Crussi, F., *The Five Senses,* New York, Kaplan, 1989.

Sacks, O., *The Mind's Eye,* London, Picador.

Lodge, D., *Deaf Sentence*, London, Penguin, 2008. (A novel, but fascinating on deafness – funny and touching.)

Brillat-Savarin, J.A., *The Physiology of Taste,* London, Folio Society, 2008. (Fascinating, a translation from the French originally published in 1825. Deals with much more than taste.)

Greenfield, S., *The Human Brain – A Guided Tour,* London, Orion, 1997. (A useful introduction.)